Hidden Struggles

PURITY, GOD, GUYS AND LIFE

Rachel Hamilton

WestBow
PRESS
A DIVISION OF THOMAS NELSON

Scripture taken from the King James Version of the Bible.

Scriptures taken from the Holy Bible, New International Version®, NIV®.
Copyright © 1973, 1978, 1984, 2011 by Biblica, Inc.™ Used by permission
of Zondervan. All rights reserved worldwide. www.zondervan.com The
"NIV" and "New International Version" are trademarks registered in
the United States Patent and Trademark Office by Biblica, Inc.™

WestBow Press books may be ordered through booksellers or by contacting:

WestBow Press
A Division of Thomas Nelson
1663 Liberty Drive
Bloomington, IN 47403
www.westbowpress.com
1-(866) 928-1240

Because of the dynamic nature of the Internet, any web addresses or
links contained in this book may have changed since publication and
may no longer be valid. The views expressed in this work are solely those
of the author and do not necessarily reflect the views of the publisher,
and the publisher hereby disclaims any responsibility for them.

Any people depicted in stock imagery provided by Thinkstock are
models, and such images are being used for illustrative purposes only.

Certain stock imagery © Thinkstock.

ISBN: 978-1-4908-0646-4 (sc)
ISBN: 978-1-4908-0645-7 (hc)
ISBN: 978-1-4908-0647-1 (e)

Library of Congress Control Number: 2013915561

Printed in the United States of America.

WestBow Press rev. date: 08/29/2013

Dedicated to
Rebecca, Emily, Susanna Williams,
Shardae Noone and Emma Young.
You mean so much to me, you are amazing and
I am so thankful that you are part of my life.

Table of Contents

Heart to Heart

*Praise be to the God and Father of our Lord Jesus
Christ, the Father of compassion and the God of
all comfort, who comforts us in all our troubles,
so that we can comfort those in any trouble with
the comfort we ourselves receive from God.
2 Corinthians 1:3-4*

L IKE ALL MY GENERATION I'M into computers big time.
A day that doesn't start with Face book doesn't seem
like a day at all. I saved up and bought my first laptop a
couple of years ago and boy was I excited to play with it. Even
though I'm pretty savvy with computers I still get surprises
as it does so much more than I at first realised. Sometimes I
think life is like a computer. I've just managed to crawl out
of the teen years which were a pretty tough learning curve
and I think I've learnt a lot about the way God has uniquely
programmed me, but I still stumble across facets of myself I
didn't realise existed.

I would never have thought of myself as a writer but
somehow the wind of the Holy Spirit seems to be blowing
my boat down a river of words. I find it weird that I, who
hid my teenage struggles from those nearest and dearest to
me am making public the deepest most vulnerable part of

my heart. Because it is the way of God to take water and make it into wine, to turn the broken vessel into an incense dispenser, I reveal to you the secret struggles of my heart. If by Gods grace I can help just one person through the lonely, treacherous valley of adolescence it will have been worth it all.

Only A Girl

There is neither Jew nor Greek, there is neither bond nor free, there is neither male nor female: for ye are all one in Christ Jesus. Galatians 3:28

WHEN YOU WANT TO MAKE a difference it is difficult to be happy with an ordinary life.

My goal is to touch other people's lives with good. Naturally this kind of attitude is not popular with the devil so he fed me the big lie that because I was a girl I was a lesser person and I could never be as brave or as strong as a guy. (This whooper is century's old but still effective.) I swallowed the lie and as it sunk deep into me I begin to hate who I was and couldn't see how God could use me with the insurmountable handicap of being a woman. It was a mystery why God had bothered to make me. I struggled with feeling second rate until God showed me that in his eyes we are not male or female, rich or poor. It was such a comfort to me to realise that God can and will use me. He not just looking for men, he's looking for a willing heart, that's what makes him smile he will use anyone who is willing. And it is so exciting when he does!

When most little girls are dreaming of owning a horse the one thing I wanted more than anything was to have a

TESTOMONY. I had asked Jesus into my heart as a young child and it was so simple it didn't seem to qualify as a REAL testimony. It was a crazy dream for a shy little girl who never stuck out in a crowd and liked to blend into the background. I didn't like strangers even looking at me and would rather be safe at home with my family than meet new people. But deep down I had a dream, a dream since I was very young, I wanted to be missionary. I wanted to work in an orphanage that would surely be a TESTOMONY. Often I would search on the internet for a missions trip but nothing ever worked out. It wasn't until I was nineteen that God opened the door for me to go onboard a mission ship for three months. I was so excited to be involved in a huge adventure and finally have a TESTOMONY.

My Testimony Part One

―――――――――⚬ᘛ ᘚ⚬――――――――――

Learn to do good; seek justice, correct oppression;
bring justice to the fatherless, plead the widow's
cause. Isaiah 1:17

I BOARDED THE SHIP THE Logos Hope" in Dubai and set sail to Sri Lanka. The nine day sail to Sri Lanka was an enjoyable time and a great opportunity to get to know fellow crew members before the ship docked and opened its doors to the seething crowds that flocked up the gang plank. Together we experienced standing on the deck with nothing but water to see, watched hundreds of dolphins jump through the waves and large water snakes and jelly fish swim by. The sun rose and set dramatically and the waves rocked us to sleep at night. We were four hundred people from fifty different countries and it was incredible to experience how beautifully the many cultures worked together. People on the ship really showed Gods love in their everyday life even if it was just with a smile or hug.

Before we arrived in Sri Lanka, I really didn't know what to expect, we had been briefed about Sri Lanka but to be quite honest I was rather scared of meeting Sri Lankan's. The first day the ship was open to the public, I went down to meet the locals on a deck set aside for it. The Sri Lankans are warm and special people and by the end of the day I felt a real connection with them. Being a New Zealander made me particularly popular as New Zealand had been playing cricket against Sri Lanka and lost. I could always count on raising an enthusiastic banter about New Zealand's inferior cricket skills. In a corner away from the cricket fans, I noticed an old lady sitting alone she looked so sad that I went to talk to her. She told me her life story and I felt privileged that she had opened up to me. Soon I met her whole family. Her daughter told me later how her mother had been very depressed but it had really helped talking with me. Back in New Zealand I had found it hard to meet people, this new courage was like a gift from God. My job on the ship was cleaning toilets, vacuuming the many stairs and hallways of the ship, and working in the laundry. The all girl team I worked with was great. We laughed and joked while working together. Cleaning the public toilets, (especially when the people who used them were not used to western style bathrooms) was challenging and a great lesson in humility.

The ship went into dry-dock during my time with the Logos Hope so we went on land for five weeks on something called Challenge Team. My first team was a group of seven people and we went to a Boys Home up in the mountains of Sri Lanka. We left the ship in the small hours of the morning and took a two hour train ride like no other train ride I've ever been on before. People were jammed in, hanging off the sides and stacked on the roof. The New Zealand health and safety officials would have been shocked. Close around me unknown faces jabbered strange words as we rattled along and yet the whole time I could feel God so close to me I never once felt frightened.

The boy's home for the first few days was wonderful and I laughed like I hadn't in years as we played games and interacted with the children. The lush mountains surrounding the tidy buildings and the pouring rain reminded me of home while the staff at the home showered kindness on me. Not all the boys were orphans some boys were there because their families could not provide care for them. Sometimes they have Parents Day and this is a very hard day for the boys who don't have any family. The day I left childhood behind forever and stepped over into adulthood was Parents Day. It was heart wrenching to see the envy in the boys without parents and know I couldn't fill that void. It was strange how well I adapted into the Sri Lankan culture. Downing spices that make your lips feel like they have melted off your face and eating with my hands came naturally. My mother says it must have been because of our family's dreadful table manners! In spite of the good work the home was doing we could feel the oppressive spiritual darkness of the land hanging over the place and many days we spent hours praying for the protection of the staff, the children and our team. I believe that we were sent there for such a time as that.

During this time I began to read whole books of the bible in one sitting as God gave me comfort through reading his word. While I was reading the boys would come up and ask me to read it to them or they would bring a bible in their own language and read it beside me. It was a special time and those children become very dear to my heart. All too soon the time came for us to leave, on the last night I spent as much time as I could with children, the older ones were very sad I was leaving, they were praying I would come back and visit, we left early in the morning to catch our train but when we arrived at the station we found there were no seats left. What would have been a big problem in New Zealand was no problem in Sri Lanka we sat on our suitcases near the open door and watched the ground pass rapidly under us the whole way back. Many people on the train came up to chat with us as we were a novelty. I didn't want to talk as so much had happened I needed time to process it all. After the crazy train ride and an equally crazy bus ride, we arrived at the venue where we were to join up with the other Challenge Teams.

Standing like an Island in the middle of a sea of reuniting friends I felt emotionally broken as flashbacks of the events, people and the cultural differences washed over me. Two dear friends saw that I was struggling and prayed with me. Looking back I truly believe that God was breaking my heart for what breaks his.

My Testimony Part 2

Let brotherly love continue. Do not neglect to show hospitality to strangers, for thereby some have entertained angels unawares. Remember those who are in prison, as though in prison with them, and those who are mistreated, since you also are in the body. Hebrews 13:1-3

THE NEXT DAY I LEFT at 3am for my second challenge team, I was not excited at all about doing another Challenge Team. This time the team was bigger and twenty of us squashed into the train for eight hours as we travelled up into the war torn area of North Sri Lanka. We arrived at the church we were staying at to find we had no beds or drinking water. We did have some showers but shock of shocks they were outside by the well and we had to develop a strange way of cleaning ourselves over our clothes (not the most efficient way of staying clean and we all ended up with the interesting experience of dirt rashes.) There was one squat style Sri Lankan toilet for the whole twenty of us guys and girls (another interesting experience). At night we strung two lines of mosquito netting over the hard bare floor and that was bed, one line for the girls and one for the boys.

Every morning we had to be up, dressed and tidied with mosquito nets dismantled by 7am to ensure we were out of the way of any church prayer meetings. As there was no food provided, every meal time we went out and brought fiery hot Sri Lankan takeaways and big bottles of water from the local street vendors. We got innovative as time went on and the boys and girls would take turns having showers with cold water from the baptismal pool (probably not the most spiritual use for it.) There is nothing quite like roughing it in strange places to bond people together. As we laughed, groaned and suffered through the showers, toilets and food, we became good friends and a tight knit team.

And then there was the transport! Our host had provided a covered in jeep made to seat ten comfortably. Sri Lankan style we crammed all twenty of us in. We were squished in tightly with people sitting on one another's laps for long trips, sometimes more than an hour. It was quite as effective for bonding as the toilets and showers, to bounce jamb packed through the big potholes in the road with a ukulele player and South African singer, who would come up with the craziest games, stories and raps. One night we were driving along, out in the middle of nowhere, when suddenly the Jeep hit a huge rock in the middle of the road. There was no way to get around it or over it. So we set off on foot to the boy's home where we were invited to dinner. With no light pollution, it was pitch black making it hard to find our way. There were some stubbed toes but looking up at the inky sky with its thousands of sparking pin pricks was huge compensation. On Easter Sunday we did a drama at church and explained to the congregation about the ship and why we had decided to get involved. Normally I would have been very frightened to do that, but God gave me so much courage that I managed to do things I would never have thought possible.

Mixing with the Sri Lankan's who belonged to the church where we were billeted gave me a real respect and admiration for how they worshiped God with their whole hearts. I have so much more than a lot of them but I am not as grateful as these people whose lives have been devastated by war. It humbled me. One day I and couple of girls from the team went to visit a girl's home across the road. These dear girls invited us in and gave us sweet tea and biscuits. Then they danced and sang for us. Between broken English and Tamil we managed to communicate. They took us to a room filled with sewing machines where the older girls made lovely hand bags to sell. These beautiful teenage girls clung to our hands telling us how much more beautiful we were than them. It was so sad they couldn't grasp how beautiful they were in their own right. The local Christians we worked alongside were the kindest people you could have meet. They have given their whole lives for their people. Many get up at 5 o'clock in the morning to go and hand out food to people so they won't go hungry. Their lives shine Gods light through everything they do. Many have faced terrible pain but have risen up and become amazing men and woman of God.

After a few days to settle in our team split into three groups, group one was the HIV/AIDs team focusing on raising health awareness. Group two were involved with children and my team was practical work. We started off cleaning a bus stop which sure needed it as it was covered in old posters and the floor was knee deep with mud. We scraped and scratched off the old posters, dug the mud out, and put an irrigation drain round the base of the shelter to stop the mud and water oozing inside. It was hard work and sometimes we worked till it was dark but it was fun as there was so much joking and laughter. Many times as we were working, people would stop and watch us. It became a real highlight to talk to the people who hung around. One day a group of Sri Lankan young men stopped and helped us clean. They said they wanted to help as we were doing something for their country. Once the bus stops were clean HIV awareness information was painted on the walls. Now they were nice to sit in and the messages could save lives

One day some of the guys were asked to clean a tube well and they asked me to go and help as I had gained a reputation for being physically strong. The well was located outside a hospital for victims paralyzed by gunshot wounds and was just a small hole in the ground not at all what I imagined as a well. To clean it we thrust long flexible tubes deep down into it and pumped high pressure water through them. While we worked, we caught glimpses of young children in wheelchairs which made me realise how much war can impact lives of even the very young. After that we went to very poor area inside a mine field and cleaned a huge well that two thousand families used to get their water. We stuck closely to the well worn path as we walked from the Jeep to the well as there was a real danger we could step on mine. It was really sad to see children who didn't have the freedom to run around on their own land because of the mines.

Cleaning the big wells was like cleaning large round swimming pools deep enough to sink a submarine in. First they dropped a pump inside the well and while the water was draining out we jumped ten or fifteen feet down into the water and scraped the sides of the well with coconut skins. Once the all the water was drained out, we dug the mud the off the bottom and loaded it into buckets that were pulled to the top on long ropes. We got out a similar way to the mud, walking up the smooth sides clinging to long ropes. It was not for the faint hearted and was best not to look down. Young people, mud and water in the scorching Sri Lankan heat, who could resist mud and water fights? Not us! We had so much fun. Getting pushed into wells, crazy rides home in the back of trucks and swimming in lakes with crocodiles and leaches, were just some of the other wonderful experiences we enjoyed together.

One day after coming back from a long day of well cleaning, there was a news paper sitting on the table, it was written in the native language of Sri Lanka, one of the Indians who could read it, casually mentioned that New Zealand was in the news. When I asked more, he told me New Zealand had been hit by a massive tornado, north of Auckland. A shaft of pain went through me. My family were north of Auckland, I had not been in contact with them for four weeks and had no idea whether they were alive or dead. With limited information it was very hard know what had happened. I was worried sick about my family, we had been invited out to dinner but the whole night I sat in a haze of worry. Its seems to be that when your down that Satin decides to get to you and this time it was no exception.

The host said something that hurt me very deeply and I sat there close to tears pretending to smile. While I was struggling to hide my suffering, I felt Gods gentle voice whisper that he was very happy with me so of course Satin was very angry with the way I was living and that is why I had been attacked That night as I washed my clothes outside in a bucket, softly crying I felt God ask me if I would give him my family. Could he take my family and would I still praise him, would I still believe that he loved me and that his will is better than mine? Would I trust him in everything, would I forsake all others to follow him? Under the Sri Lankan moon I gave God the most important thing to me, I gave him my family and I put my whole trust in him, giving him control of my life. The next morning I found out that the tornado had hit nowhere near my family and everybody was fine. Then I knew God had allowed me to go through that time to get me to fully trust him. Everything comes to an end and it was time to head back to the ship. The pastor's wife had made us sweet tea to start our day. Although we were sad to say goodbye to our new friends we were excited about catching up with ship mates back at the dock. We were also very excited about a REAL shower after using an outside bucket for two weeks. We joked about how there was two things that we were going to do back on the ship, have a shower and lie on a REAL bed.

To see the ship again after five weeks was like coming home. There was much hugging and laughing as all the teams reunited. We all had fascinating stories to exchange. While it was great to be all together again I found the first few days back on the ship difficult, I longed to still be on challenge team where every day was an adventure and your never knew what could happen. I also missed being able to just spend time with the Lord, life on the ship was very busy, as we worked from 6am till 3.30pm but I felt like I wasn't really making a difference. We were supposed to sail to India once we got back from Challenge Team but the ship still needed more work done on it so we stayed two more weeks in Sri Lanka. I was glad as I had grown to love Sri Lanka and its people. Working everyday with people from all over the world expanded my world view and taught me a lot about different cultures, while the two Challenge Teams had expanded my friends. It was nice to wake up every morning and be able to chat with like minded people over breakfast, lunch or dinner. I stood on the deck the night as we left Sri Lanka watching the port that had been our home for nine weeks, get smaller and smaller.

I had come to make a difference in the lives of the people of Sri Lanka but it was actually them who made a difference in me. Their gentle simple kind way of living had taught me more than any bible Collage or famous preacher could. Through them I saw the true power of prayer, real servant hood and the treasure of gratitude for everything. It was exciting to see India for the first time, with only a few days left before I was to fly home, I felt blessed that God had fulfilled my dream of seeing India even if only for a short time. The ship opened for the public and soon there were long lines of Indians patiently waiting to board the ship. One day I went down to deck four to connect with locals and suddenly from out of nowhere lots of wide eyed children crowded around me wanting me to sing, dance and talk. I was quite the celebrity. There was a sweet fourteen year old girl. She sat next to me in a quiet moment and told me of her hopes and dreams of one day travelling abroad. As she left she begged me to never forget her and I sure haven't.

The time onboard the Logos Hope truly changed my life. The last night was hard to say goodbye to dear friends I had grown to love deeply. The memories that we share will always be in my heart. The strange thing about happiness is it is best obtained when you are too busy trying to help others to look for it.

What Purity Means

What Others Say

I don't have a wow answer nor do I know THE answer but I personally think that purity means setting your heart right before God. To always pursue God's heart and to have a heart that beats like His. Not to say that we can ever be like God but the process of always keeping your heart clean for the Holy Spirit to stay.

~Rachel~

Purity is respecting and obeying Christ and being accountable with yourself and Christ. Purity is a priceless virtue to have it is respecting yourself, respecting your husband, respecting your God.

~Anonymous~

Purity is remaining free from anything that deters or hinders your relationship with God.

~Why-Wont-You-Wait~

Purity is not only physical, it's also emotional. It's very important to guard your heart and not give it away prematurely. It's very easy to go to extremes regarding topics like this, by "guarding your heart" I don't mean you're heart should be callused . . . just careful.

~Andra Jimenez~

Purity is not just abstaining from immorality but also abstaining from doing or saying anything that would cause others to stumble

~Evan~

Purity is living a chaste life

~Edin~

Purity is a lifestyle of refraining from actions that will tempt you or another person to fall into moral failure.

~Rebecca~

Purity means cleansing your heart, beginning with a love relationship with God and letting everything else flow from that.

~Allie Kay Iolley~

Purity means having a heart for God. Matthew 6:21

~Peyton Wilpolt~

Purity means living a life free from contamination, accepting Christ's justification and redemption from the past and then living by God's standards.

~Tinashe Nyahasha~

Purity means having a clean loving and caring heart, respecting Gods wish by not sleeping with someone before you are married, respecting your body and heart.

~Ana Trochez~

Jesus instantly comes to mind when I think of purity. I think purity means "without sin". Jesus is the only one who was entirely without sin, because he was God! Since we were made in his image, the only way we can be complete is to be pure like he is! He encourages us in Matt 5:48.

~Lianna Joy~

Purity is a state of heart in which, your heart aligns with God's heart.

~Waiting for your Boaz~

Purity means abstaining from sin in order to keep holy before God,

~Austin Abernathy~

Purity means keeping yourself free from sins that harm your innocence,

~Emily D~

Whenever I think of purity for myself, I always say "if God was right next to me in person would I be doing that."

~JR~

I think purity ultimately stems from understanding one's identity in Christ. God calls us to be holy as He is holy, and that flows through not only our physical lives, but our mental and spiritual lives as well. It's one thing to be pure of body, but if hatred and anger are festering in our hearts, I think we've missed the meaning of living a pure life before God.

~Aysha Gerald~

Finally, brothers and sisters, whatever is true, whatever is noble, whatever is right, whatever is pure, whatever is lovely, whatever is admirable—if anything is excellent or praiseworthy—think about such things.—Philippians 4:8— This to me is purity! It's submitting your heart and thoughts to Christ!

~Cherish~

Purity means keeping all of yourself pure before God.

~Colette~

To me, purity means remaining unstained from the world, keeping blameless and holy in the sight of God and man, and presenting yourself to Jesus as a pure vessel, waiting to be taken as His Bride.

~Julia Grace~

Purity is when the person is right with God and living how God wants them to.

~Ruth England~

Purity is about being pure in everything we do, what we eat, read, watch and think. Being pure in everything makes us closer to God. When you are pure there's no guilt or shame and you will have self respect. When you're pure you'll be an effective witness for Jesus.

~Chimwemwe~

Praying

Pray without ceasing. 1 Thessalonians 5:17

I F LIFE WERE A CAKE, prayer would be the baking powder, without it everything is flat. When I was a little kid my prayer life was restricted to bedtime shopping lists. But by fifteen I began to have a closer walk with God, that was the age when faith in God became my own not just something I believed because my family did. I vividly remember the night God showed me I was a very selfish person and that he wanted me to put other people before my selfish desires.

I started praying for friends and family instead of just using prayer as a wand to get the things I wanted. It was a turning point in my life. What is amazing is when God gives you an answer to prayer I saw this in a special way when I was praying for someone to go with me on my mission trip. The whole time leading up to the trip, I had been asking God to put the right person in the seat next to me on the plane. Then a week before I left, another New Zealander applied to go on the ship. The best I had hoped for was pleasant strangers in the seat beside me for each stage of the journey, but God answered with a companion with the same destination, age and heart as me.

We met at the Auckland airport just before we flew out and I was amazed to discover I knew her cousins. Sarah has a great personality and by the time we had lived through hours of cramped seats, aeroplane meals and endless waiting in foreign airports we felt like we had known each other for years. She has become a wonderful dear friend to me and we still keep in touch. After all, who else remembers the smells of Sri Lanka, cleaning swaying ship toilets or prayer meetings late at night outside on the top deck of the ship. Another thing God has challenged me about is praying for the person I may one day marry. Have you ever thought about praying for your future husband? I don't mean being totally preoccupied by dreaming and praying about him all the time. But praying that if it is Gods will for you to marry that God will protect and watch over your future husband. You never know when he might need prayer. Pray for wisdom in relationships that God will revel to you who is a man after Gods own heart. Pray that God will lead you to the right people. Also ask God what he wants to teach you right now, in this time of singleness. God is not some scary God, he is a loving, compassionate, caring God, who is slow to get angry and is deeply in love with you! You don't have to be amazing at praying, you don't even have to pray really long prayers. He just wants you to talk to him like you would a best friend, just chat away naturally with normal words. It doesn't have to be fancy or hard, make short little arrow prayers an essential part of your life and prayer can be a piece of cake.

Precious Pain

The sacrifices of God are a broken spirit: a broken and a contrite heart, O God, thou wilt not despise.
Psalm 51:17

MY GRANDMA COMES UP WITH some rather strange presents at times. It's exciting because you never know whether Christmas will bring something wildly exciting or very strange (like the time Dad got a plastic back scratcher and two bags of dried beans. My brother was not very pleased the year he got kitset dolls furniture but I thought it was cool. Each little hutch dresser or chair came pre punched on a flat sheet of balsa wood. All you had to do was break out the pieces and slot them together and suddenly you had a little table. God fingered my teenage years just like that little table. He broke me apart and put me back together. If balsa wood had feelings I guess it wouldn't enjoy the necessary process of punching and breaking and like me would for a time have lost all joy. Depression and suicidal thoughts weighed me down. The devil was trying to kill me, make me believe that I was worthless and of no value and God did not step in and stop him. Everything seemed to be crashing down on top of me. Why God was letting me go through so much pain?

Broken friendships lay in peaces around me. The dreams I had for my life seemed shattered and often at night I felt forsaken. It seemed that as soon as I managed to cope with something difficult God would give me something else to deal with. I struggled to balance study and volunteer work at a local camp for children while dealing with emotional pain. My grades began to drop and often I would end up crying out to God in the bathroom at lunch time." I can't take this any longer." I'm not one to talk about difficulties I'd rather sweep them under the carpet. I put on a fake smile to avoid having to explain to people the pain I'm going through. I think "They won't understand." So I stuff it deep down, try to act tough and be the strong one, but really I'm dying deep down inside.

No one knew the extent of my difficulties, not even my family. The worst part was 'The Terror.' I was sixteen the first time it happened, the presence of the evil one in my bedroom with me. Almost every night I was plagued by terrifying nightmares and oppressed by an unseen but ever so real force that pushed me down on my bed until I felt my life was being forced from me. Something was out to get me, to kill me, to destroy me. Crying out the name of Jesus was the only thing that got me through those hideous nights I felt crazy, I doubted that anyone would understand what I was going through, people would think was I nutty and I should be locked up. I become detached from the world and alone as each morning I woke up feeling physically and emotionally tired from the nightly struggle. I pretended everything was ok to those around me, even though something was terribly wrong. It got all too much and I couldn't deal with it so one day I got a knife and put it to my arm, I just wanted to cut the pain out from inside me to let it pour out and give me relief. I pushed the blade into my arm but something stopped me. It felt good, too good in a dangerous way. So I stopped and never again tried cutting.

I fell into deep depression, I hated myself for feeling depressed, I wished that I could be normal like the people around me, happy and carefree but I couldn't be, locked in my prison.

I began to struggle with suicidal thoughts and hated myself even more. Here I was a good Christian girl from an amazing Christian home, with Godly parents and yet I wanted to end my life. What kind of a sick person was I? I held so much fear, guilt, shame and pain inside me. I hated who I was and desperately wanted to be someone else, someone different, someone God could be proud of because how could he be proud of me a broken and useless person. I thought my suffering was unimportant because I knew many people have been through worse things and I hated that I hurt and hated that I felt emotion. But like the lovely father he is, God helped me see that he was proud of me, he didn't think I was failure for struggling in fact, he saw me as someone brave. He showed me that my suffering matters to him and that I don't have to always be strong, I don't have to do it alone.

Just when it felt like I could almost cope, the bullying began. The bully was a childhood friend who I loved very dearly and I still don't understand why she turned on me.

She changed from friend to enemy in a moment with hateful searing words that caused me to go outside where I could be alone, put my head on the ground and scream and scream in emotional agony. That was just the beginning as text bullying started hounding me with frequent horrible messages that came day after day for a very long time. I wondered if she would ever give up.

I had tried being the very best friend I could be, but it wasn't good enough I became very depressed and withdrawn from life and people thought it was odd that I was so quiet

No one knew I wanted to end my life and it seemed like even Jesus expected me to be strong alone. Finally I told God "that's it! I can't take this anymore, change my life or I don't want to go on and God in his mercy answered that cry with the mission trip. It lifted me out of myself and brought a new joy and hope into my life. I would not like to go through that time of life again but in the same way the balsa wood took on a new dimension and usefulness once it was put back together so I feel I have comfort and insight to offer others because of those tough years God allowed me to struggle through. Certainly I was not ignorant about spiritual darkness when I encountered it in Sri Lanka as I had already served an apprenticeship in fighting with the devil and knew the power of the name of Jesus Christ. The bible says God disciplines his children and nobody enjoys the process but afterwards it yields the peaceable fruit of righteousness. The refining fire of sorrow and suffering while unpleasant has the power to develop a whole new dimension in our lives if we keep holding onto God and that makes it precious pain.

Suicide

*For I know the plans I have for you, declares the
Lord, plans for welfare and not for evil, to give
you a future and a hope. Jeremiah 29:11*

THE TEENAGE YEARS ARE STORMY seas and just when
you feel you have climbed out of a deep trough and
are breasting the wave your, friend falls in and the
world goes black again. Can anything affect you more than
a close friend committing suicide? Even though I knew she
had wanted to take her life, it shook me to the very core when
it did finally did happen. I had tried really hard to be there
for her but I felt I had failed her. How God let this happen?
Could I have done more so this would not have happened?
The pain was so deep and the guilt felt so real. I couldn't see
how God could bring anything good out of this situation? I
was so sad it seemed impossible to smile again? Over time
the sadness has lessened and although the loss of my friend
is still great I value the important things her life taught me.
I want to reach out to the broken, to share my story to with
hurting people and spread the message that everyone is loved
and important. That suicide isn't the answer. I know some
experiences mark you forever but God can turn something
horrible into something beautiful that blesses others. He has

brought me out of the ashes and given me back my joy. He has convinced me he will never leave or forsake me. God wants to bless you too and he has a special plan for each of our lives.

When my family and I were visiting the USA, we went at work for a week at a place for people who have been abused or struggle with some kind of addiction. We went for a few days to help out. As we worked in the gardens and chatted with people over mealtimes I began to see how strong these people really were. Some had made bad mistakes but they were willing to admit it and say "I can't change my life on my own, I've sinned and I want to change. I need Gods help." It takes great courage to admit you are weak and that you can't do it on your own. I admire them. Since starting up an online ministry for suicidal, depressed and hurting people, I have met so many brave people. They are going through so much and very often feel they are failures because they feel so much pain. But the truth is, it is brave to journey through suffering and not give up. God has a plan for this misery and difficulty. He is not an unkind God who loves to see us suffer. No! He wants to heal you, to use you in astonishing ways. He sees your brokenness but he also sees your future and says there is no sin too enormous for forgiveness.

He doesn't love you less because you sin more than that girl over there. NO! He says "I can see past your sin to the person I made you to be and have a hope and a future for you!" Your value doesn't rely on anything you have done, and is not lessened by what others have done to you.

Dare to believe you are a loved and costly jewel in the eyes of God. Sometimes I cry "Why God are you letting me go through this and I forget that there are things that God is blocking and saying, "No I will not let Rachel go through that". I forget God is protecting me from things I don't even know about. Just as he cares about me, God cares about you and what you are going through, and is looking after you even when it feels like he doesn't and has given you too much to handle. Strength is more than just being physically strong. You may not be able to move a muscle in your body but still be stronger than the strongest man in the world. Inward strength is something that we can only have if there has been suffering and hardship in our life. Physical strength is showy, inward strength is usually hidden but both types of strength are developed through training and patient practice. It's not surprising it is difficult to obtain physical or emotional strength as nothing of real value comes easily. All of us at some point feel that if God truly loved us then he wouldn't let us suffer and he would hasten the arrival of the dreams of our heart. After all he has the power to do all things so why do we have to live through hard times. But it is the oyster with the irritating grit in its life that produces the valuable pearl. A very deep trust in God can be the fruit of hardship, waiting, tears, and difficulties if we surrender the suffering to Jesus. It helps to view troubles as training and a chance to start storing up treasure in heaven. And even though it often doesn't feel like it, Jesus is right beside you, holding your hand helping you through. Suicide is NEVER the answer.

Purity In Danger

What Others Say

Listen to the Devils mouth. If you do, your strength will seep away and not only will you lose the courage to fight you will lose the ability to do so.

~Ruth Hamilton~

The easiest way to put your purity in danger is to decide not to value it. The world devalues purity.

~A Teen Girl's Heart~

It is dangerous to compare your path of purity to the world's standard of what is normal.

~Jenn Rosario~

The most dangerous thing for purity is conformity, using the world's values to define you.

~Rachel Sophieanne~

The most dangerous thing you can do if you want to stay pure is to surround yourself with individuals who have no desire or intentions of living a pure and holy lifestyle. It's time that we as young people are honest and avoid what tempts us. My temptation is not alcohol or drugs instead its attractive men, and I've fallen thinking

I was spiritually strong. I now realize that its Jesus who gives us strength and the Holy Spirit who guides us in all truth not man. I was honest to myself and because of that Jesus has cleansed me and made me whole.

~Shanaya Sykes~

Don't put yourself in situations where you know you may be tempted. The best way to prevent temptation is avoid being in places where you struggle.

~Taylor D~

I think the most dangerous thing people can do is place your heart in someone else's hands. Sharing everything you hold dear, your memories, your dreams, desires and fantasies at the deepest level with someone you are not married to can lead you into a false sense of security and may cause you to stumble.

~Rachel Nip

It is dangerous to think you are strong enough on your own. Everyone should realize they need a Saviour every day and that they need to be accountable to someone. We are human and therefore can fall if we consistently live close to the edge of temptation.

~Tinashe Nyahasha~

Turning your focus away from God (even for a moment), can be detrimental to purity. Idleness opens up opportunity for sin as well.

~Lianna Joy~

I believe putting yourself and heart in dangerous situations is not good, the bible says "above all things guard your heart"

~Waiting for your Boaz~

To intentionally be in tempting positions is very dangerous. Also to not rely on God is doom for your purity because your own strength won't be enough to withstand temptation

~Austin Abernathy~

It is dangerous to play with fire. Sometimes we overestimate our will power and believe that because we are still pure in an area if temptation presents itself to us we will always overcome. We are not relying on God by doing that.

~Cynthia Castillo~

The biggest danger comes when we remove the guard from our hearts. The Scriptures tell us in the book of Proverbs, "to guard our hearts, for it is the wellspring of life." When we become complacent and lazy, we're not on guard for the things that could hurt us spiritually. That includes the movies we watch, the music we listen to, the friends we hang out with and where we spend our money. The list could go on for days but it all comes down to this, is what I am doing honouring to my future spouse, and is it honouring to God? If the answer is no, then it's something to flee from immediately. All it takes is a glance to corrupt the heart, and the enemy wants nothing more than to bring us down. Don't give him a foothold.

~Aysha Gerald~

It is dangerous to lose sight of the importance of guarding your heart! I can't stress it enough! Guard your heart!

~Cherish~

The most dangerous thing is to not set boundaries or stick with them or seek God's guidance.

~Colette~

The most dangerous thing you can do to put your purity in danger would be to walk away from God. If you are not right with Him then you are not right.

~Ruth England~

Waiting Game

Wait on the Lord: be of good courage, and he shall strengthen thine heart: wait, I say, on the Lord.
Psalm 27:14

ONCE UPON A TIME IN a land far away, there lived a rug maker. He made the most beautiful rugs in the entire kingdom. He had two lovely daughters and he knew that each girl secretly wished to have her own rug. So one day he called his daughters and said." I know each of you has a secret wish to have a rug. I will make each of you a beautiful one." As you can imagine the girls could hardly sleep at night while they waited for their father to finish their rugs. One day the girls were taking some food to their father that their mother had prepared for him. The oldest girl arrived before her sister, and she saw a corner of the most beautiful rug sticking out from underneath the door that led into the back room. Suddenly she knew she could not wait a minute longer, because that rug was meant for her. She ran to the door grabbed the edge of the rug and pulled.

Little did she know that it was not finished she wanted it before the time was right. After much pulling she had freed the rug. It was more beautiful than she could have imagined. She did not seem to see the tare and a tiny rip that had been made from pulling it out from under the door. She went home overjoyed. The younger sister knew that her father had a rug for her too and she wondered why it was taking so long to finish. She went to the rug shop and found the corner of a beautiful rug sticking out from underneath the door just like her sister had. She couldn't help but wonder whether it would be nicer to have it now rather than waiting for it because waiting seemed to take so long. She decided to trust her father and wait even though it was hard to do. At long last the day came when her rug was ready. She made her way to the shop. The door was open and her beautiful rug was lying over a chair. The wait had been long but worth it. The rug was made of bright colors, had many details and was quite perfect not a rip anywhere.

Many years after the rug maker was long gone, the daughters still had their rugs. The oldest daughter put hers in the kitchen where she loved to admire it. She loved it but not with all her heart. The younger daughter's rug was tenderly put in the best room in the house. She treasured it and loved it will all her heart. Waiting is hard but always worth it.

When I was seventeen, guys really scared me and I was much more interested in studying than boys. But by nineteen things had changed and I told God "I'm ready for the next part of my story." I was keen to see the rug made for me! I tugged at the rug under the door at night through my begging prayers but the reply was a firm but loving "Not yet"

"O.K God."

Then I met a boy whom I really liked and I wanted him to be the one. I hoped one day he would notice me. "If he likes me then everything will be perfect" I thought. But the small quiet voice at the back of my head kept saying "He's not the one, you haven't yet met the person you will marry." How I cried thinking that I had to be hearing wrong. But God kept nudging me "Give him up, stop holding on to him." Slowly

I surrendered to God. It wasn't easy and took time but I did it. Then shock of shocks the boy showed interest in me. It was my dream come true but it didn't feel right. The joy I thought I should be feeling just wasn't there. My eyes opened and I was so thankful God had said no about this boy. I've learnt when God says wait or no, it is in our best interests to obey. So many of my peers are getting married or engaged and I would be lying if I said I didn't care, because I do. I want to have someone special too. I admit sometimes I feel like giving up and settling for second best. It would be easy to settle for some of the guys who have shown interest in me. They are Christian guys and nice enough but not right for me. If I ignored God's No I would be in danger of not only pulling the rug out from under the door prematurely, I would take someone else's rug and we would spend the rest of our lives trying to make our unmatched patterns blend. I wish I could say I'm a saint and never wrestled with God's will, but the truth is I struggle every day especially with this waiting bit. What is it about waiting that is so hard? We want to run ahead, speed up the clock and jump into the future instead of enjoying the present. Sometimes I complain to God it is just "Too Hard." And he always tells me the same thing to "just hold on a little bit longer, it will be worth the wait." And I have to say, the older I get the easier waiting seems to be getting. A few years ago if you had told me I would be happy to be single at twenty one I would not have believed you. The single part maybe but happy, could single people ever truly be happy? And yet I am happy, very happy with my life and I am so thankful God has not bought someone into my life yet. These last few years have been the best and worst of times. They have been essential years of getting to know myself and learning to trust in God. I can even say these painful turbulent years have been the most fruitful of my life. When I was sixteen I didn't know how people in their twenties could cope with singleness but now I am here it is much easier than when I was a teenager. Back then I wanted someone to fill up the void of my identity I didn't realise at the time that they were great years to find out who I was. God protected me from a premature relationship that would have stunted me from getting to know myself. I am still waiting for my custom made rug. I can't even see a corner peeping out from under the door. I have struggled with impatience like the older daughter but now I am content to wait and trust my heavenly Fathers perfect timing and like the younger daughter I will value my custom made treasure all the more for waiting.

Waiting for God's best.

I will wait for the best, and never give in. I will wait in till God say yes, then I will run with arms open wide. I never give up on Gods perfect will. No matter how many years go by I will stand firm. Hold to the promise that God has my best in sight. God and me together, never apart, when I long for love I know God is right here, holding me close. God is holding my heart in-till it is time. It's crazy to say but waiting's ok, so I will wait till I meet you someday, and you will know I kept my all for you.

The Devils Lying Lines

Lest Satan should get an advantage of us: for we are not ignorant of his devices. 2 Corinthians 2:11

"IT'S ABNORMAL TO BE TWENTY one and not have even told a guy you like him" a nasty little voice whispered in my ear. "You are too slow to get going, look there is a single man he will do. Hurry before it's too late." The voice had a horribly convincing sound to it, but then the devils voice always sounds horribly plausible whether it speaks in our head or spouts forth from friends and family member's lips. The most painful talk I received from human lips was the one where I was told I would end up bitter and alone because I was not willing to market myself. I would LIKE to have a go at marketing myself. It DOES fell like God is slow, and I am often tempted to take control and write my own story! It is hard to resist taking things into my own hand and the devil is right at my elbow urging me on to impatience with his many lies. He's not even urging me to do terrible things just anything except obey God. I wanted to uncover his lies and find out what he's been telling others so I asked a lot of people online the question. "What do you struggle with, what are lies the devil tells you over and over." Here is some of the feedback I received.

"Singleness means you're undesirable and unloved."~A Teen Girl's Heart~

"Everyone is immoral and society accepts this."
~AnnieTrochez~

"You're missing out on something good". ~Juliee~

"Be like everyone else, enjoy lustful pleasures because there are no good guys out there, no one is striving to be pure."
~Jess Lacy~

'You are not good enough no man will ever want to be with you because of who you are." ~Erika Paloma Lopez~

"You might as well have live together before marriage, you are going to get married eventually and you're already committed to each other." ~David Donegan~

"That HE is not out there and you will grow old alone."
~Cheri Joyner~

I encounter the lies through friends who imply "I am nothing without a boyfriend, I can't possibly be happy single and it's time I started looking for a man." ~Raelynn Russell~

"I am not pretty or smart enough. Dating and breaking up is a normal part of life." ~Carolyn Krolick~

"Why waste your time on things that will never come true, you have tried and failed, why not relax, there is an easier way" ~Shiku Simon Tobe~

"You are not good enough; you are never going to be enough, for God or anyone." ~Gabrielle Kinnish~

"I need to search for a husband, to feel complete, to feel loved." ~Lisanne Slotman~

"You can't attract the opposite gender." ~Patience Sibanda~

"You are not forgiven, you will never be different or worthy of a godly man." ~Brandy Reed~

"You are all alone." ~Jennifer Passet~

"You have wasted your life so are worthy of nothing." ~Carolina Mukami~

"God has forgotten you and is not faithful." ~Tiffany Langford~

It is easy to see the Devil has been busy with everyone not just me The first step to resisting his lies is realising we are not the only ones who struggle with feeling alone, discouraged and hopeless Feeling unattractive and out of step with the world is a normal feeling for many people. It helps me to know I am not the only one to struggle with these lies. Next time he tells me it is abnormal to be twenty one and never told a boy I like him I will say loudly "shut up Satin."

Is Purity Just A Physical Issue?

What Others Say

Great military victories always start with great strategies. If you do not bring the intelligence of your mind and conviction of your heart to the battle for righteous living, you will never conquer your flesh.

~Ruth Hamilton~

Purity is more than just abstaining. Anyone can do that . . . Saved or not . . . It's having a pure mind and heart. Purity is about having sin's residue removed from the heart.

~Generation31 ~

I believe that purity affects the heart and mind because we are spiritual beings.

~Shanaya Sykes~

Purity is most definitely hard work. We work on a daily basis trying to live in the Spirit. The devil is always after us, tempting us to give into our fleshly desires, impurity being one. With the battle constantly raging, we have to be on our guard at all times. "Fruit it out, don't flesh it out."

~Taylor D~

Purity affects both the heart and mind. If your body is contaminated, it definitely affects your heart and mind.

~Maria Leite~

1 Cor 6:20 says we don't own our own bodies, God does. The same goes for our hearts and minds. Because he owns us, we must honour God with our entire being (Deut. 6:5), not only our actions.

~Lianna Joy~

Purity affects you physically, mentally, emotionally, and spiritually.

~Waiting for your Boaz~

Purity affects the heart and mind first, then it affects the physical. A lot of things happen in the mind before they are done in the physical. Your mind has to be pure before you can LIVE pure.

~BFA~

Purity is definitely a whole body issue, heart and mind included. If you are a virgin but go online and look at the wrong things or listen to bad music you're not being totally pure.

~Emily G~

It affects your heart and mind because once you get physical you want to be physical even more and it alters the way you think, and it ultimately affects your morals.

~ActualGodlyGirl~

Purity definitely affects the heart and mind. Evil is born in the heart and that impurity will latch itself onto other areas of our lives and spread like cancer. In a way, physical impurity is a mere reflection of the inner impurity of our hearts and minds. When our heart and mind are attuned to the heart and mind of God, impurity of the body won't stand a chance.

~Aysha Gerald~

Little things have small beginnings! Guarding my heart and mind is paramount! I cannot expect to remain physically pure if my heart and mind are unclean.

~Cherish~

Learning To Love Yourself

You are altogether beautiful, my darling; there is no flaw in you. Song of Songs 4:7

I STARED AT THE GIRL in the mirror, how I loathed her, why did I hate her so much? What had she ever done to me? Why couldn't I just love her for who God made her to be? In common with many girls growing up, self worth was a huge issue. I look a lot younger than the rest of my peers and during my teenage years I hated it. My mum has always said that looking younger than you are has advantages when you get older, but when you are fifteen and old ladies ask you if you are ten it is not a convincing argument. Who wants to be offered the kids colouring competition at the library while your peers seamlessly blend in with the adult world. I grew older on the inside but my years were very slow showing on the outside. At the age when you most want to be thought of as older, more mature than you are, I was seen as a little kid. I used to look at myself carefully in the mirror every day, was it my hair, my clothes or the baby fat round my face that made me look so juvenile. "The chubby cheeks, yes that must be it" I would decide.

I began exercising hard to try and lose some weight so that maybe, just maybe I would look older, then I might be pretty and boys my age would notice me instead of thinking I was some primary school pest. It was hopeless, I never could lose weight and looking back I am thankful it wasn't possible as I wasn't overweight and I could have easily developed an eating disorder. So the years ground on, sixteen, seventeen, eighteen, nineteen, twenty, still the well known words hounded me,' "No way, you look so young; I thought you were half that age!" Even more deadly were the times when people mistook me for a boy, and any thread of self love disappeared the day when someone called me 'It'.

"It is very hard to tell if IT is a boy or girl", the words haunted me for months after. Was I a freak of nature, God must have made a mistake when he made me. The devil socked me with lie after lie. "Who would ever think you are beautiful?" "Who would want to walk next to a freak like you Rachel?" "You will never get married." "Don't even bother looking in the mirror you will hate what you see." Lie after lie plagued my mind. God didn't plan for me or you to have a miserable image of ourselves like that. He wants us to know that we are made in his image. He never makes mistakes and he didn't goof up when he made any of us.

I thought that if guys didn't show interest in me that meant I was ugly, that I wasn't as beautiful as the girl that had all the male attention. It took me a long time to see that if I judged my worth by what others thought of me, I would always be insecure. God saw me as beautiful in his eyes because he made me perfect just the way I am, I needed to let that truth sink deep into my soul and judge myself from his perspective. You are beautiful, no matter what lies the mirror tells you, no matter what people have told you. You have such amazing worth because you are a unique individual. Don't get caught up comparing yourself negatively to others. The perfect face and figure are prone to fashion fads. If you are not considered a beauty now, cast your eye over international beauty queens of the last hundred years. Every face and body type has been a beauty in some country at some time.

Physical beauty will rapidly fade, who you are deep down inside never will. I know some old ladies who radiate a special attractive glow. Their spirit is so kind you just want to be around them, that kind of beauty never goes out of fashion. We can all develop that inner beauty if we yield to God. The devil loves to set up little standard cardboard cut-outs that we can all compare ourselves to and feel inferior to. It's a very nasty highly effective game he has been playing since the beginning of time. It's like giving all the citrus trees in an orchard, pictures of pear trees and suggesting that because orange trees are shorter and have orange coloured fruit they are very inferior to tall pear trees. Of course he gives the pears trees pictures of grape vines and tells the pears they are big and gangly with dry insipid clumsy fruit compared to the delicate flexible dainty grapes. It's all designed to destroy you, and if you buy into the devils lies they very well could destroy you. God however loves you and wants to bring you to a place of freedom where you accept yourself for who you are including the bits you like and the bits you're not so keen on. It is your choice who you listen to. Are you going to co-operate with the Devils nasty little game or accept Gods definition that you are a beautiful, unique individual created in his image!

Your Inner You

But now, this is what the Lord says he who created you, Jacob, he who formed you, Israel: "Do not fear, for I have redeemed you; I have summoned you by name; you are mine. Isaiah 43:1

DEBBIE SAT ON HER BED and looked discontentedly at her diary, "another day and nothing notable to enter as usual". Will I ever be a 'Somebody' like the popular girls at school she wondered? Surely I would be a worthwhile person if I had a job, a boyfriend, over a million followers on Twitter, a thousand friends on Facebook. I need something more in my life I so I can be a 'Somebody.'

We all crave significance and want to be considered worthwhile people. It is a mistake however, to think like Debbie, that significance is defined by what we have, what we do or who we have hanging off our arm like a handbag. I met a boy while travelling overseas. He was a very Godly and wise young man, different to the other young men I knew. He really attracted me and made me feel worthwhile. But same old story God said no and added "just because he is an amazing man of God does not mean he is the best one for you. Just because he is husband material does not mean he will marry you. Find your significance in me not another person." If like me you meet an amazing man and it doesn't work out like you had hoped, don't think you are not worthy of a Godly husband. Remember just as there are many apples in the world there are many men. If the one you set your heart on was not part of Gods plan for your life there will be another far better for you at a better time if you leave it to God. You are worthy of God's best but that may not always coincide with what you think is best. It is a smart move to give such an important area to someone who is all knowing. There is a certain kind of apple that looks red and juicy and fabulous on the outside. It is not until you get close to the core that out find out the middle is rotten. Even among the true apples there is a big difference in flavours. Some are sweet and some are tart and sour. Some people like the sweet varieties and others like the tart ones. If you choose an apple that turns out rotten or not to your taste it's no big deal but if you choose the wrong man it will make your life uncomfortable at best and devastate it at worst. Fortunately God doesn't have taste in people and favourite children. God loves you for who you are. His love is not based on what you do or how much you have. He sees the good and the ugly we keep hidden inside and there is nothing you have done that will make God love you less. You are more than your past sins. You are a loved and cherished daughter of God. Your scars don't define you neither does God want you to define yourself by the sins you have committed. He wants to give you freedom and a new beginning. He is a God of second chances he can make you into a woman worth waiting for. As we wait for Gods perfect choice for our lives it is easy to forget that some man will also be playing this difficult game of patience. We need to focus on becoming a woman worth waiting for. And just who is a woman worth waiting for. She is one who understands that a male heart is just as breakable as a female one, and treats with respect the heart of every male she meets. She has given her all to Christ, he is her first love and she is doing whatever he asks her to. She knows who she is in Christ and does not need a guy to feel she is of value. She respects herself and those around her by dressing modestly. She knows her weaknesses and looks to God for her strength. She is more interested in developing her skills so she will be better suited to help her future husband than dreaming about a man who will fix all problems. She knows a real man is not all strength. She is very much her own person with hobbies and dreams. She has embraced her singleness and is content where God has put her. She isn't afraid to stand out. She doesn't need the things of this world to satisfy her, because she relies on God to fulfil her. She doesn't need a man to define who she is. She can live without him but she chooses not to. That is a woman worth waiting for and a very worthwhile person.

Dare to De Different

And be not conformed to this world: but be ye transformed by the renewing of your mind, that ye may prove what is that good, and acceptable, and perfect, will of God. Romans 12:2

WHEN I WAS YOUNGER IT was very important to me to win peoples approval, I wasn't like the others. I longed to fit in and be normal. I longed for acceptance. I thought if people liked me then I would find fulfilment, but it always felt hollow. I was asking for something that friends and family could never give me. Deep down I was crying out for something only God can ever give us, unconditional love. God's unconditional love is so powerful it breaks the chains of self and teaches us to live for something beyond ourselves. When we live for something bigger than ourselves, when we give our all to Christ, we find our lives become rich. Making a stand can be terrifying. Choosing to stand apart from the world can be very uncomfortable, I have always been one of those people that would much rather hide their light under a bushel. Jesus told me I should shine from a hill top. "Who me, the shy girl", surely he didn't mean me? I would much rather just fit in and not make any waves. Suddenly God was asking me personally "what do you stand for?" Was I just going to go along with crowd or was I going to say, "I stand for you no matter the cost." Slowly I began to let go of my image, to stop worrying about what other people thought of me.

I put more energy into pleasing and standing for the one who loved me enough to die for me when everyone else would have given up on me. I always wanted to be that extroverted girl, the one that was never at a loss for words, the life and soul of the party. Many nights I would cry into my pillow wishing that I could be different. I failed to see how God could use me, the quiet girl who was named The-Silent-One at Collage. I didn't see till much latter that God could use me to reach out to the ones that didn't fit in just like me, to touch the lives of people who otherwise would have been overlooked. The very things that I hated about myself, were given to me for a special purpose, they were part of Gods plan for my life. Is there anything you hate about yourself that you are always trying to change but can't? Look at it carefully. God may have set you aside for a unique purpose. The very things you fight against might qualify you for a special mission.

I have always interacted with people a lot younger than myself. All through my teenage years I was much happier playing "Duck-Duck-Goose" than hanging out talking with my peers. Many times I struggled with the feelings of being odd, immature and silly. It wasn't until I worked at the Boys Orphanage that I saw God has given me this gift to touch children's lives. I began to fully embrace it as part of who I am and I was able to connect with the boys in a way I never could have without it. So learn to love the things that make you uniquely you. Never despise something you love to do, just because it doesn't fit the boxes of what other people think. Dare to say I love me for me. Dare to be different, dare to stand apart from the world.

Is Purity Just about Marriage

What Others Say

Purity starts in your mind. Your mind is the battlefield. That's where decisions are being made.

~Gea Slotman~

You don't jump into a marathon before you've trained for it. Marriage is a lifelong battle for purity and faithfulness. If you don't train your heart and mind for it now, don't think for one moment you'll manage it in marriage.

~Ruth Hamilton~

Purity encompasses more than just marriage. Individuals can be married and still impure. It should permeate every aspect of our lives not just the physical area but also the inner heart of a man or woman.

~Shanaya Sykes~

I believe purity can and should be applied to every area of life.

~Tinashe Nyahasha~

I do believe purity can be applied to every area of our lives, not only marriage.

~Waiting for your Boaz~

Purity can absolutely apply to every area of our lives!

~Emily D~

I definitely think purity drives deeper than marriage. Every area of our life is affected by our choice of whether or not to be pure. While being pure of body for our future spouse is a beautiful thing, there must also be purity weaved through other areas of our lives as well.

~Aysha Gerald~

I definitely believe purity is important in all aspects of life. Whether it is waiting for the husband God has for you, or hanging with friends, purity needs to be shown in your life. If someone is gossiping about another individual and you listen, does that defile you? Absolutely, to be pure in every situation is to represent Christ in all that we do and say.

~Julia Grace~

I think purity is meant for every area! The Bible is my standard, Psalm 119:9: 'How can a young person stay pure? By obeying your word.

~Lisanne Slotman~

Purity can be applied in every aspect of our life not just marriage and dating.

~Ruth England~

When Your Role Models
Let You Down

It is better to trust in the Lord than to put confidence in man. Psalms 118.8

T HAD BEEN A FAIRY tale wedding, the bride glowed, the groom was dashing and the dress was breathtaking. But Sophie couldn't help feeling that something was missing. Maybe it was Alice had been the girl everyone looked up to, the role model all the girls wished they could be like. But Alice was getting older and didn't want to be single so she settled for a nice enough non-Christian man. Sophie was scared, if the very person she looked up to couldn't go the hard yards what hope was there for Sophie.

I couldn't believe my ears could it really be true, the person that I had looked up to and wanted to be just like, had settled for a lot less than Gods best for her life. She had decided to give up waiting on God to act and accepted an ungodly man. Did she believe the lie God had forgotten her? She had been the one who taught us younger girls to stand for what's right, dress modestly, wait on God, yet she couldn't follow through herself. Just like Sophie I wondered how I could live up to a standard my heroine had failed to maintain.

People are going to let us down, it's part of life. What are our standards based on, God or some human authority? It hurts so much when our heroes let us down and disappoint us. It can make us insecure, afraid we will make the same mistake because we thought so highly of that person. It can be hard to forgive those who let us down. Many tears I cried over the fall of my role model. Her demise however taught me the valuable lesson that we never know who is looking to us as a role model and how far our influence for good or evil extends. I doubt my heroine knew my name but she impacted me. I want to do all I can to live a life that encourages those around me to reach for the higher goal. I will let people down because I am certainly not perfect, but even our imperfections can inspire others if we stay surrendered to God. Being let down by people has taught me to make Jesus Christ my role model, he alone will never let me down. He is perfect and all his ways are right. So look to him, he will never disappoint as he is the very best role model and hero to have!

The Pity Party

In everything give thanks: for this is the will of God in Christ Jesus concerning you. 1 Thessalonians 5:18

I WISH I COULD SAY that I never struggle with self-pity, but the truth is I am one of the worst offenders. I am one of those people that tend to see the melancholy side of life. The day I let self pity consume my life was a dark day. I didn't fit in, which seemed a problem worthy of sadness. I felt sorry for myself and wallowed in the idea that no one would take any interest in me. I never thought that God might be using this time to teach me to reach out to others instead of focusing on myself and waiting for someone to be friendly to me. He was trying to teach me to be others centred but I was far too busy hosting my own private pity party.

Then one day the light bulb went on, God wanted me use the pain, sorrow and unhappiness I was sunk in and turn it into something good, to use my experiences to see other peoples pain and to reach out to them. When I stopped looking just at myself, God started using me to touch other people's lives. There is something so joyful about helping others. Even giving a stranger, directions how to find a street imparts a warm feeling. Reaching out to others doesn't mean I have never had to battle with self pity again, but it has helped heaps. Of course, to cry and feel pain doesn't always mean you are in self pity, don't feel that you should never cry or show emotion. I have been down that path too and it's just as unhealthy. There are times when it is important to grieve and crying is part of the healing process. The problem is when we become bogged down, fixated on our self, going round and round like a CD with a repetitive glitch. Like everything in life God wants us to have a balance, we need be able to distinguish between self pity and real pain. If you are unsure whether you are in self pity or not, here is a little tip. Be really honest and ask yourself "is there a little bit of enjoyment in this misery and do I really want to let it go?" I have found that self pity is quite fun in a strange way and that is its biggest danger.

First Love

—◦◦◦◦◦◦—

But seek first the kingdom of God and His righteousness, and all these things shall be added to you. Matthew 6:33

E VERYONE WILL HAVE ENCOUNTERED THOSE baby toys that kick round houses where a small person lives. The bright orange and blue hollow ball covered with geometric holes designed for the thrilling occupation of slotting triangular or cross shaped blocks into the corresponding holes. Frustrated is the infant who insists on trying to swash the square block into the hexagonal hole. If we try to slot a man into the God hole of our lives we will end up more frustrated than the persistent baby. No matter how wonderful or how godly a man is, he will never be able to fill the void that only God can. It was hard for me to understand this when I was younger I read about it in books but I wanted a person to hold my hand, to hear a voice say I was beautiful, that I had worth. I thought if a young man took interest in me then it would be God's way of showing me he loved me. I forgot that God doesn't need a middle man. He wants me to know him first without the distraction of someone else. Many times I would cry in frustration, didn't I deserve love as much as anyone? Eventually I understood God wanted to give the purest sweetest love there was, if I would only let him. No man could ever full that God hole and I shouldn't expect him to.

When we place young men higher than God, we put unreasonable exceptions on them, they are only humans and will never completely understand us the way God can. They were not made to complete us nor we them, rather we complement one another so we can spur each other on towards the high goal of pleasing God in every area of our lives. Deep down guys are just as insecure as us so don't lay unrealistic expectations on them. If you want a perfect prince, run to Jesus. When we place a man higher than God, he will fall short and disappoint and we will always feel like we are missing something. So I urge you dear sisters, put God first in your life, make God your number one and he will fill that void in your life. Then when you marry, you will be able to love you husband with a sweet love, not a needy love, but one that is safe in the Lord.

Like my Mum always says "husbands are wonderful but they would make terrible gods." You will never get a perfect man just as you can never be truly perfect. Neither will you be fully content and happy with a man until you have first given your heart to Jesus Christ who is perfect. He holds the universe in his hands like a huge ball. If you fill the God slot in your heart first, all the other blocks will fall into place.

Defining the Concept of Purity

What Others Say

The preservation of your purity is essentially a statement on your sense of self worth. You are worth so much more than an empty, one night stand or a casual relationship. You are worth true love. By standing firm and waiting for real love, you make your worth known to the world.

~Ruth Hamilton~

Purity is being unsullied by sin or moral wrong. This is unmistakably the most important virtue, because without it you can never acquire other virtues. Purity of heart is being yourself and blooming with the same colours in the middle of the wilderness when no one sees you.

~Charmaine Garcia Anac~

I think physical purity is important because it shows your spouse that you loved them enough to wait for them. That nobody else gave you what they gave you. It shows your spouse that yes it was hard but they were worth the wait.

~Rachel Nipp~

Purity is a determined effort to live by Biblical standards. It is a daily choice and it is progressive. While no one is totally pure, we should increasingly become more pure by daily practicing purity. Purity is important because it frees us from the bondage of guilt, self condemnation and fear of discovery. It enables us to have a smoother relationship with Jesus.

~Tinashe Nyahasha~

I believe the concept of purity is important to individuals because it shows a lot about where you stand and your state of heart.

~Waiting for your Boaz~

Purity is to keeping yourself from anything unclean and is important because it keeps us from pain. God doesn't want us to bring pain to ourselves so He wants us to stay pure.

~Cynthia Castillo~

Not only is purity scriptural and moral, it guards your heart. As a Christian you should guard yourself and save yourself.

~Taylor~

Don't allow yourself be conformed in this dark world, this is purity's concept. Purity is very important because it reflects what you believe, your morals, behaviour, and conduct.

~Francesca Dominique C. Jimenez.~

The concept of being pure is very important because we're made in God's image. We're not trash, but divinely made. It protects you from a broken heart and a lot of pain and broken dreams when you stay pure! Also it saves you from some horrible diseases!

~Lisanne Slotman~

Purity is God's will for us. I define the concept as keeping your heart, mind, thought life and body where God wants you to be.

~Ruth England~

My Way Or Your Way

To do what is right and just is more acceptable to the LORD than sacrifice. Proverbs 21:3

"GOD HAVE YOU FORGOTTEN ME" I cry. "No darling" God whispers back, I have you just where I want you to be,. It's going to be ok." I lay surrounded by my team of sleeping girls, it was day two of the kid's camp and something just didn't feel right. I couldn't put my finger on it but I felt something was missing. The first few camps I had helped with, had been great, but this time was different. I had been studying that year but still managed to find time in the holidays to be a team leader. I wanted to make a difference, wanted to show someone I cared. What I did not realize at first was the thing missing was the most important ingredient of all. God had moved and it was time for me to let go of the old patterns and follow him onto the next stage he had in store for me. But I wouldn't listen, I stubbornly clung on to what I thought was the most important thing for me to do. No matter how wonderful, worthwhile and important something is, if it's not what God wants you to be doing right now, you are not living up to your highest calling. This was so hard for me to understand. So I held on to the good but not the best.

Fortunately God loved me too much to let me stay in that place. By simply pushing the pain level up he made the camp more and more uncomfortable until I got the message loud and clear. Where did that leave me? Staying at home with my family, reading the bible and learning to hear Gods voice. This seemed like a waste of time but in hind sight if I had not let go of being a camp leader, I would still be leading teams of kids every school holidays and I would never have thought of going on the mission trip that changed my life. The good can be the enemy of the best. Are you holding on to something good that you suspect God may be asking you to let go? Pray carefully about this because God may have something new in store for you.

Sometime later I was thinking about becoming an intern for a year-long missions outreach. It was everything I wanted to do and I longed to be part of it. The organisers were flatteringly keen to have me involved and it was travelling to places I really wished to go. At first I was just really excited about the opportunity but as I continued to pray about it I had a persistent uneasiness that nagged at me and as the uneasiness grew stronger every day, I had to conclude it wasn't what God had planned for me, so I let it go and felt peace confirm my decision. What God gave me instead seemed a rotten deal. He let me go into a situation for five weeks that was very dysfunctional, where I was over worked and emotionally abused until my very self worth was threatened.

Was this God's will for me? Yes, I believe it was, and although I would never want anyone to go through that kind of experience, I wouldn't trade it for anything. I learnt much about the dark side of human nature which has given me insight and empathy for people in hard situations which I draw from every day in my current ministry. Even though it was very difficult, there was an element of peace surrounding me because I was in the centre of God's will and it was all part of his training program for me. Sometimes what God calls you to do can sound crazy to other people, just remember God has called us to extraordinary things and don't get discouraged when others around you scoff, God will bless you for following and obeying him even when it's hard.

Learning To Hear
Gods Voice

I will instruct you and teach you in the way you should go; I will counsel you with my loving eye on you. Psalm 32:8

T IS POSSIBLE TO EXPEND a lot of energy on a rocking horse. But all that energetic brisk movement is getting you nowhere. So often we fill our lives up with busyness. We believe that if we work hard enough we might gain the approval of God and others around us. So we bury ourselves in what we believe is important. But no matter how important, no matter how worthwhile anything is, we will never find fulfilment until we realize God's love doesn't hinge on what we do. He loves us no matter what. This is hard for me to write because I always want to be out there doing something big and important. During my life there have been many things I have pushed in my own strength. I was so worried about getting a career because I don't know if I will ever marry, I wanted a job to feel safe and secure. However, job after job fell to the ground and amounted to nothing. I rocked furiously on my rocking horse of life missing the point that God wanted me to be still and listen to what he was trying to teach me. My sister is such a great example of this as I have watched her put her trust in God not herself. I have been like Martha rushing around trying to earn Gods love through deeds. She has been like Mary sitting at his feet listening and obeying him, no matter how strange it may look. She has shown me the true and beautiful meaning of trusting God. Sometimes God does the most in our hearts when we least expect it, it is often when we feel useless that God is working deep down in our hearts.

I rush here and there trying to get everything done, stressing myself out because I have so much to do. Suddenly I stop, why am I rushing about, why am I trying to do everything in my own strength? God wants me to rest in him, to stop doing it in my own strength but instead lean on him. God will carry me; he will help me get everything done if I trust him. Deep down I fear I am not good enough, that if I don't work hard and give 100% I am a failure. If I rest for a moment I am weak and everything will fall apart and it's my fault. But God wants us to stop for a moment to show us it is ok to rest, it is ok to not have every part of your life together. It's ok to have a messy room. It's ok to take time for yourself. If something falls apart when you are resting it's not a disaster, you did your best. Your best will do, don't burn yourself out, trust God he has it all in control even in the times we rest. Through stillness, God teaches me contentment, helps me work through unresolved pain and draws me closer to him. Treasure the quiet times, draw closer to God as he draws closer to you. Don't be like me rocking furiously caught in the trap of being Martha rather become like Mary. God wants to teach us to stop labouring in our own strength, to stop for a moment and rest in the shelter of his wings, to see that sometimes it's ok to do nothing but listen to God voice. A slow moving snail will take you further than an energetic rocking horse.

Walking The Path
Less Travelled

But small is the gate and narrow the road that leads to life and only a few find it. Matthew 7:14

WHEN I WAS A CHILD my mother would shop at a place called Junk and Disorderly, no I am not kidding that was its name and it sure lived up to its name. Stuffed to bursting with anything from the normal old chairs and tables you would expect in a second hand shop through to the quirky stuffed possum and ceramic bedpan you did not. You had to climb over broken prams and shoe scrappers as you made your way through the shop. To the untrained eye the shop was full of worn out stuff, but to my Mums loving eyes it was full of many treasures which she carried home in triumph.

To the casual observer junk and disorderly may be a perfect description for many of us. God however is eagerly searching through the mess for the greatest of all treasures, a heart that is willing to obey him no matter what. If you possess a heart like that, and are following Jesus closely, there will be a lot of people who will mock you for the road that you are taking. The Devil will not just let you walk down that road carefree. Oh no, he will be on your case more than ever, trying to break and discourage you while whispering lies in your ears and you will be attacked in the areas that you are the most vulnerable.

But don't be afraid, God is looking down on you and smiling, saying there is my daughter, she is doing the hard yard and I am so proud of her. Giving God the first fruits of your life isn't always fun, sometimes it feels like you are doing hard work and struggling while people around you seem to be cruising through life. It can feel like you are missing out on the fun, missing out on life. It can feel like you are trying so hard but not getting anywhere. When you plant a garden you can't just sow seed on the hard ground and expect to pick strawberries the next day. First you must dig the soil deep and break up all the big lumps. It is hard slow work. Your hands blister, your muscles hurt and you sweat in the sun. It is easy to look over the fence at your friends growing vigorous wild grapes over their septic tank while they sit in the cool shade, and wonder what's wrong with you. Why are you going to all this effort with nothing much to show for it. How well you work will not show up until the harvest. If you are ploughing your ground well there are going to be times when you feel a failure, that you are not doing anything of value.

There will be times when you feel like no one sees what you are doing and you feel like giving up, When it all seems just too much. Keep patiently digging this is just the blisters talking. The teen years and early twenties are your foundation years, get the foundations right and you avoid a lot of problems in later life. Fortunately ploughing does not last forever. And remember, sour wild grapes only look impressive until you have to eat them.

How Important Is Modesty Really?

―――――――――――――∽◌◍◍◌∽――――――――――――――

Let us not therefore judge one another anymore:
but judge this rather, that no man put a stumbling
block or an occasion to fall in his brother's way.
Romans 14:13

WHEN MY MOTHER WAS SMALL Junk and Disorderly didn't exist so her Grandmother would occasionally take her to a gift shop down the road and buy her the treat of a 'Lucky Dip. There were always two bins, one for boys and one for girls filled with knobbly small brown packages. For two dollars you could plunge your hand into the depths and pull out a mystery package. The excitement lay not so much with the junky little plastic dog or vase she got, but the excitement of the unknown.

We tend to think of modesty as wearing a sack, something shapeless and ugly, that modesty is something that we are forced to do as Christians. For a long time I felt strange because I didn't wear revealing clothes like others my age. I knew it was the right thing to do but I also wanted to fit in. It wasn't until I got a bit older that I began to see modesty is to be prized rather like the special wrapping around Christmas present. Modesty is respecting and valuing yourself enough to say "I have more to offer a man than just my body. I am a girl worth fighting for." In respecting your body you respect God and everyone you meet. Modesty is valuing who God made you to be and helps godly young men stand for what is right. A guy is free to see you as a person instead of getting sidetracked by your body.

The really sad thing about dressing immodestly is it lowers the standard of man who will be interested in us as the godly ones assume the worst about us. It also makes us seem needy and insecure. Dressing modestly can be scary; it's daring to stand apart from the world. It is brave and radical and doesn't mean you always have to wear a dress. While I think we should know how to enjoy wearing skirts and dresses it is more modest to climb a ladder in jeans. Not all shorts are immodest either. I think that we need to look at our clothes and question "does this top show too much, are these jeans a little too tight?"

Modesty doesn't mean that you have to dress like you are in a cult, it means dressing to protect yourself. Ask God and a man you trust to show you if there are clothes that need adjustments or getting rid of. Modesty doesn't have to be an old fashioned thing. You can wear very trendy clothes modestly. You just may need to tweak them. A very short low cut dress can become cute and modest with jeans and a top underneath it. It is so hard for our brothers in Christ in this society; let's help them as much as we can. Besides as my mother says,

"If you cover up well, not only will guys respect you but they will imagine everything far better than it really is just like a Lucky Dip!"

HERE IS WHAT GUYS SAID ABOUT GIRLS WHO DARE TO BE MODEST.

Because the opinions of guy are very important to girls, I asked for some feedback on the subject of modesty and here what I got.

A modest girl respects herself, and isn't a conformist. ~Josh Collins ~

When I see a girl dressing modesty, she shows respect and integrity, and she's looking for someone serious with the same qualities. ~Josbel Nazario~

I appreciate her decision. Considering how lustful thoughts come naturally, I appreciate anybody who doesn't encourage them. ~Joshua Nason ~

Modesty is attractive! It shows a woman respects herself. ~ToMyLovingWife~

Modesty is extremely important. Honestly, I think modesty is incredibly attractive. Both men and women should be modest. Guys don't need to show their muscles and ladies shouldn't show too much. ~Michael Germain~

WHAT OTHERS SAY.

I feel like modesty is of utmost importance, for both guys and girls. We don't know whose (future) spouse we might encounter. ~Sierra Palacios~

Modesty is clearly not just about your clothes. It's about your actions too. ~Anonymous~

I think it's not only physical but also emotional, and sadly nonexistent in this generation. ~Rebekah Caldwell~

I think there are two types of modesty: clothing & actions. Clothes mean covering yourself even if you have a body to show off. Actions are synonymous with humility. Keep modest with awards or prizes by giving God the glory. ~Hadlee Hamner~

Modesty is about respect (For me, my boyfriend, & brothers & sisters in Christ). I don't want to make anybody stumble. ~Bekah Mundt~

I think modesty is very important, because it reduces lust. ~Actual Gentlemen~

The right kind of godly guy will love your modesty ~Hannah Patulski~

Modesty is one of the most important things a preteen girl needs to learn. it also applies to guys when in high school. ~Beth Schuman~

For me modesty is both how you dress and how you act. If you dress modestly but act provocatively then it's not helping. ~Emily Diehl~

Ladies, if you want to find a guy who wants more than your body keep your body covered. ~Tips4ChristianTeens~

Modesty is a way to show love for our brothers in Christ. ~Jαψδεη ΚεRRꝉ~

I used to use the phrase "modest is hottest", but we shouldn't be striving to be "hot", we should be striving to be classy. ~Megan Marie~

Boys fall in love with your heart, not your body and how "revealing" you can be. Don't make it harder for a guy to keep a pure mind. Dare to be the one catching the guys with your smile not your body. ~Chloe_H~

So let's make modestly the new normal and believe we are worth respecting. Modesty is extremely beautiful. God wants you to see this and believe it. Though modesty may be unknown to a lot, it is a protection and guard. Yes it makes you stand out as different but it's the right kind of different. You may attract less male attention by dressing modesty but the ones who notice you will be the kind of men worth waiting for.

What Christian Guys
Want Girls To Know

Do not sharply rebuke an older man, but rather appeal to him as a father, to the younger men as brothers, the older women as mothers, and the younger women as sisters, in all purity.
1 Timothy 5:2

TO ALL CHRISTIAN WOMEN, YOU are a gift from God. That alone says you are beautiful. Another point, don't ever settle for second best! As a man, I almost did but God led me away from her because HE knew there was someone better. Lastly, I want Christian women to know that men do pray for their future spouse. I pray for my future wife everyday and ask God to bless her and continue to strengthen her relationship with him. If my future wife happens to read this one day, I want her to know one thing: trust God and continue to stay on his road because as our relationship with God grows stronger, the closer you and I are to meeting and together we can encourage each other to be more like Christ. ~Michael Germain~

Know God for yourself then you can really be a help mate.
~Richard Jay~

I would like girls to know that guys were not all the same.
Give us a chance and get to know us. Be friends with us
those who are friendly and those who are real men. I would
like girls to know that some of us men like to start off being
friends at first. I for one, love to treat girls like princesses &
queens. ~Bisantino Anthony~

Dear amazing girls, please stop dating piece-of-trash boys. It
makes us sad. If you complain about never finding Mr. Right,
stop trying. Give Mr. Right the chance to find you. Ladies, he
will treat you like he treats his mother and sisters. Ladies, you
need to understand that there is a perfect guy out there for
you. He exists and he's dying to meet you. Hold out for him.
Look at yourself in the mirror before you leave your house
and ask, "What kind of guy am I going to attract looking like
this?" If you throw yourself at the first guy who gives you the
time of day, you're going to miss the one who will give you all
his time. Are you looking for someone to listen, protect you,
and give you everything you need and more? Try trusting God
before searching for that guy. ~A Northern Gentleman~

We're still out here! We might be rare, but Christian gentlemen
are out there, if you look & not settle for anything less.
~Christian Gent~

I would like them to know that even though Christian guys
have the mindset of Purity-Over-Lust we still need help from
the girls too. We need them to keep us accountable, not
tolerate lustful actions, to maybe take charge and keep us on
track. If a girl shows a guy her beautiful heart it will help him
to not to focus on her beautiful body. ~Alex Christian F. ~

That no relationship will ever be perfect, it's about two hearts connecting, equal yoking and balance. ~Josh Collins ~

Relationships shouldn't be fully governed by the guy. We actually want the girl to lay down some rules also. Take charge. ~Chris Blankenship~

If you have something to say don't beat around the bush or hide things. We can handle it. No lies, no secrets.~Christian Man~

I would like Christian girls to know we're all a family in Christ you are our sister! ~To My Future Wife~

A real man loves to take care of his wife, pay attention to her and spoil her. ~ToMyLovingWife~

They should know to have a relationship with Christ alongside a relationship with their lover. That is the strongest team. ~Jesse~

We're interested in girls who are interested in God. The more she pursues God, the more we'll pursue her! ~Young Man's Struggle~

We want a woman with self respect, an opinion of her own grace, who expects to be treated like a lady. ~Tinashe Nyahasha~

Whatever a girl "shows" a guy stays on his brain like a tattoo, impossible to remove. Save it for marriage. ~David Donegan~

As a Christian guy I want a girl to know she should be sold out to God, seeing things from the perspective of God's word, believing in His word. Girls should be helpers like Sarah was to Abraham. They should understand the importance of growing in their relationship with God they will always make progress towards God, because they are God's vessels in bringing life into the world. ~Ganiyu Tairu~

I want them to know that they are not objects, they are beautiful creations. We would love it if they fear God and preach the truth. We want them to use discernment about whether we are for them or not and we want them to care about God more than us. It's sad when some of them talk about the heart but they judge guys on appearance. When they wear a short skirt or a low top they give us a bad picture of them. We love it when girls are modest, the fancy way they charm us when they dressed not for eyes of men but for the eyes of God. We love each one of them as sisters and we want them to grow, and submit to God in every area. Test everything, hold to the truth and love God more than us. A girl who fears God is more than a Victoria's secret model, there is no comparison. ~Edher Cavero~

Girls don't give up hope finding godly men. They do exist. ~Joseph~

As much as Christian men (or men in general) hate the idea of rejection, we want women to know that it is still our responsibility to take the risk and don't want the women take the lead in initiating a date/relationship. Our prevalent popular culture has it all mixed up. We are Boaze's in our own right. One of you could be our Ruth. Until then, put yourself out there (like Ruth did), so we can notice your God-given uniqueness, character, and beauty. We'll take notice and pursue you "Put yourself out there" meaning there's a very subtle thin line that a woman can do to let the guy know that she's interested but still let the guy take that risk of rejection. I'm no expert in dating or relationships, but when women dress modestly and have a strong foundation in Christ that gets my attention, that's what makes me stop and take notice. ~Chris Evangelista~

Guys who are looking for a physical relationship target girls who dress like they are asking for one. So be modest and dress not to attract but rather, dress attractively. Though the word beauty is more associated to ladies, I guess this one can also be applied vice versa. Guys like the real deal, they like someone who's authentic and is not hiding behind what she thinks people want to see. We are also much more blown away to see a lady who is confident in her identity in Jesus Christ. ~Jordan Zapanta~

Guys that have true relationship with Jesus are attracted not to your physical appearance but to your spiritual maturity. And don't give romantically attached meanings to all the things that guys do. Christian guys often get misinterpreted when they show concern for their friends. We ought to be nice because we have a responsibility to you as our sisters in Christ. ~Ronnel Ramos~

Girls, don't think that you have to be someone else to be loved by someone because the truth is, you are loved. You are all princesses and daughters of a King named Jesus." Girls, for now treat guys as your brothers. Wait for the right time when you can treat someone as your future husband. The right thing at the wrong time is still the wrong thing. ~RM Rodriqguez~

Don't try to change us or the way we are, because God is the only one who has the authority and power to change us. If you want us to change, you also have to change. And please don't have the mentality that a woman is our weakness. Not all boys are like Samson and David because first and foremost, as a Christian guy, our only role model is Jesus. Please don't conclude that we like you unless we really spelled out that we like you. And in terms of communication, we have feelings and we are not insensitive. We just don't really get or understand what you want to point out because there are words that have only one meaning for us as a man and have many meanings for you as a woman. For example, when girls say "I don't want to", you put many meanings to it like "Chase me, ask me again, etc" but for us boys, we only interpret it as, you really don't want to. ~Mark Soriano~

Not all boys will take advantage. Some are really sincere in their intention of pursuing godliness. ~Paul Placer~

Your support for us as sisters is enough to make us think and do well in our tasks. Don't think we ever want to compete with you. Honestly, girls have many bright ideas but to boost our spirits as men, it would be great to get support from you. ~Arvick Mirondo~

Love List

But my God shall supply all your need according to
his riches in glory by Christ Jesus. Philippians 4:19

H AVE YOU EVER SAT DOWN and thought about the
things that are important to you in a man? Or is just
getting a guy the only thing that you think about?
Anyone about to buy a car would have some basic idea of
the sort of car they wanted. The size and style would need to
reflect their needs. A family of eight who live in the country
will need a very different car to a single city woman. A big
family who bought a little red sports car because it was
cute, fast and red would quickly end up frustrated because
it is totally unsuited to their needs. If it makes sense to have
a general guide line when you go to buy a car how much
more should we have some idea of the values and qualities
that are important to us in a potential husband? Many girls
caught up in the magical' wow-a-guy-likes-me' moment have
picked a sports-car-male when what they really needed was
a minivan-man.

A while ago I was challenged by a friend to write a list
of the qualities and attributes I wanted in a man. He said
that he had written a list of what he wanted in a wife, even
down to colour he wanted her eyes to be. He was amazed

when he met her for the first time to see how God had heard his desires even down to small details. Don't get me wrong, I am not saying that if a man has blue instead of brown eyes you should conclude he definitely isn't Gods choice for you. However, I do believe it helps to have a check list to remind us what truly matters in a future husband? When I was younger it didn't matter who the guy was, if he should show an interest in me it was enough. Who really cared if he had the same values as me? I was so insecure I felt if no guy showed interest in me that I wasn't truly a girl. Now I am a bit older and the novelty of crushes has worn off, a more mature mindset has taken its place. I am more focused on things that really matter. Does he have the same depth of faith that I have? Are we going in the same direction in life? Do we have compatible intelligence and personalities? Instead of getting caught up in the maybe-we-could-fall-in-love mentality I see there are much more important things to worry about than a bruised ego. This has stopped me getting side tracked by young men that don't have the qualities I want in a husband. There have been times in the past when I was keen on someone only to find on closer acquaintance they didn't have the qualities I was looking for. Now days I have a pretty good idea straight away if God is saying no about a guy I like. It is saving me a lot of emotional energy. Some people believe that I am too fussy but I believe with all my heart that God can bring me someone with all the qualities I have on my list, if that is his will. So I encourage you to make a list of the qualities you want in a man, write it in your journal, hide it away and watch God do amazing miracles because God can give you the desires of your heart. But also remember God may change your desires. Be excited God has amazing things in store for you far more exciting than a new car.

Mythical Milestones

He has made everything beautiful in its time. He has also set eternity in the human heart; yet no one can fathom what God has done from beginning to end. Ecclesiastes 3:11

MARY COULDN'T WAIT TO HAVE a man. The excitement of dating, flowers, chocolate, first kiss and changing her online relationship status all seemed so desirable. There was just one small problem she wasn't allowed to date until she was eighteen, and at fourteen that seemed a million years away. Finally her eighteenth birthday arrived. "Expect to get a wedding invite soon." She told everyone at her party." But there was a little problem she hadn't meet that special someone yet. The months rolled by, "I'll be an old maid" Mary cried as nineteen loomed on the horizon. Luckily a young man had recently moved to her church. Within a few weeks they were a couple and on her nineteenth birthday with her friends gathered around, she walked down the aisle. "Now no one can call me an old maid" Mary sighed with relief.

Some birthdays mark more than the passage of time. They are gateways to previously denied activities such as going to school, driving, drinking alcohol or voting. The danger is attaching romantic expectations to certain birthdays. Many times I have heard "I want to marry before twenty five, I am allowed to date at eighteen," the list goes on. This is dangerous because we unintentionally put God in a box and set ourselves up for disappointment. We have left ourselves no mental flexibility for a slower time frame and are more susceptible to settling for less than Gods best. It is easy to be so worried about being alone, we become desperate and ready to take anyone. The teen years are unique valuable years. It is possible to miss out on the things God wants to teach us now, because we are so worried about our future and finding someone before it is too late. Gods timing is often not the same as ours, so laying down the "Age" will help us become much more accepting of where God has us now. If you are meant to marry God knows the best age for you. If we remain single longer than we expected, we are not old, unwanted, ugly or weird. God's timing is not ours He is never early, never late but right on time.

Is Purity Easy

What Others Say

Purity requires hard work because its not easy to overcome temptations and guard yourself.

~Dammy~

Anything at all that is of God requires hard work. That's because Satan is a fierce opponent and he's going to take you down anyway he can. If you pledge your heart to purity Satan will declare war on you.

~Ruth Hamilton~

In a world where purity is basically looked down upon, it'll never be easy. But, it'll be easier if you make it a priority.

~A Teen Girl's Heart~

Purity does come with hard work. Take it from someone who isn't pure. I got off my walk for a time. Purity is something not to be thrown away. I pray every day that God gives me His armour to battle Satan and his temptations and I've been able to do that for over two years.

God has truly blessed me with getting to know Him more and more every day. My walk is stronger than ever and it will continue to grow.

Remember, Christ was tempted if he can overcome it, then we can as long as He is guiding us!

~Michael Germain~

Living a life of moral purity is a journey that is broken down into days. Each of those days is broken down into the moment-by-moment choices that we make. We have all the power, resources and help we could ever need available to us in Christ – but the choosing to walk in that power is up to us.

~Charmaine Garcia Anac~

I believe that purity does require work. In life there are different temptations that come our way. I cannot say the work is hard because I believe when we give our burdens to God he gives us a way to maintain purity. I have found once I've decide to change things became easy because I want to live holy. The temptations are still there but I chose not to give in. If I had chosen purity but still hung with friends who didn't believe in that choice, then the work would be hard. Nevertheless none of us can get purity by ourselves, it's in the blood of Jesus. We just have to accept it and let him lead us into the path of holiness and purity.

~Shanaya Sykes~

Purity can most definitely be applied inside and outside of marriage. Your body is a holy temple of The Lord, so to honour your body before marriage is to honour Him.

~Taylor D~

I believe purity requires work. It takes the renewing of your heart and mind everyday!

~Waiting for your Boaz~

Purity requires so much work, especially for a guy. It is a constant battle that over time even begins to physically wear you down because when Satan sees you making that stand he throws everything he's got your way. Without God it is an impossible war, but with God its can be a hard fought victory.

~Austin Abernathy~

Purity requires hard work, and sometimes you can be made fun of for it. But I think it is very important.

~Emily D~

It requires hard work because as much as we try to walk in our faith, we're still human and we're still flesh.

~Taylor~

In my own experience, purity is EXTREMELY hard when you're trying to do it on your own. God's strength is something I've come to heavily rely on, because without it, I wouldn't stand a chance at being pure. Every day I slip and stumble, but every day, His grace runs deeper

~Aysha Gerald~

Purity is work, but it's like working a muscle that doesn't get much use. The more I work it, the easier it becomes!

~Cherish~

Purity requires work, determination, and commitment. Temptations need to be resisted.

~Colette~

I think it requires hard work! For me it's not easy to every time choose God instead of my flesh. It has been very challenging already! I really think an intimate relationship with God is the key to stay pure.

~Lisanne Slotman~

Purity requires hard work. One must pray and with the LORD's help keep every aspect of our thoughts and life pure before God.

~Ruth England~

The Fantasy World

Those who work their land will have abundant food, but those who chase fantasies will have their fill of poverty. Proverbs 28:19

SALLY SHUT THE BOOK AND leaned back in her chair, "what a wonderful story of love, betrayal, and handsome heroes". She thought about the part when then the hero saved the princess from drowning. "I can't wait in till my prince comes and sweeps me off my feet. It will be just like my favourite fairytale." she thought happily. She imagined the moment HE would first hold her hand, the moment HE would pull out the diamond ring. And (sigh) the moment (captured on film) SHE would walk down the aisle. It was all so wonderful, also amazing, all so in her head.

Be careful with romance books and movies. They can make you discontent in your singleness Yes it may be thrilling to read a book you just can't put down. The movie may be so beautiful it brings tears to your eyes. But we must be so careful what we are feeding our minds. Why are there so many romance books and movies? Because deep down in the heart of a girl (no matter how much of a tomboy she is), there is a deep desire to be really known and loved for herself. We all want to be special to someone. We all want to be chosen and hear the words "she is mine and I love her." This desire is God given, however when we become obsessed with romance books and movies we are sliding down a dangerous slope. If Sally keeps day dreaming about her own imaginary fairy tale romance she could quickly move from feeling dreamily happy to very discontented when her own Prince Charming fails to turn up at an expected time. Or if he did turn up, maybe she wouldn't recognise him in the form of ordinary Bill Blogs. And worst of all she could squander her precious unattached years mopping over her single condition instead of trusting in God and making the most of the opportunities marriage and small children would limit.

When we envy the girl in the movie, the princess in the book, we can fall into self pity. We forget Hollywood over plays the romantic side of the special relationship between a man and a woman. Not all men are going to send you flowers and chocolates, or swoop in on the end of a crane and save you from a giant lizard. When we fill our minds with a heavy dose of unrealistic romance it puts huge expectations on Bill Blogs who will never be able to live up to Superman and Mr Incredible. I am not saying that you should never watch a Chick flick or read romance books; we just need to be cautious about what we are letting into our minds and what our focus is. The danger of fantasising is it takes you away from reality, it drains your life. Instead of getting out and living life as it is we waste time dreaming about an imaginary perfect life. While this can be fun it is a terrible trap. It is possible to get so caught up in the world of make believe we forget to live in the present. It is possible to think too much about the physical side of marriage forgetting it is only a small part of married life. Knowing someone as a person and understanding how they think and who they are deep inside is much more of an issue. We need to give our heart to Christ not some fantasy man we have made up in our head. Our hopes, dreams and desires should belong to God so we can say "I give you control of the romantic area of my life, make something beautiful out of it, I know your plans for my life are far better than anything in a book or on the TV."

The Battle of the Mind

*Casting down imaginations, and every high thing
that exalteth itself against the knowledge of God,
and bringing into captivity every thought to the
obedience of Christ. 2 Corinthians 10:5*

H E'S SWEET, CARING, KIND AND thoughtful,
he would be perfect for me" thought Hannah
as she looked across the room at James who
had just started coming to the bible study. Hannah wasn't a
flirt and she didn't throw herself at guys, she was part of the
churches 'Young Woman waiting for God best in a husband'
group, she hadn't even been on a date before. Single and
waiting she always told people but inside she was really just
waiting for James to notice her, "Thanks God I'll have him"
she prayed silently as she watched the dark head bent in
prayer. I know when I was growing up there were times when
I said I was single and not interested in anyone but inside my
head I had built a fantasy around someone I liked. I thought
"maybe he's the one". Like Hannah I built imaginary castles
on nothing more than a silly crush. I didn't want to let go and
say I will not fantasy date, I will be single, truly single, I will
wait for your best God or I will not marry.

When we fantasy date we can become attached emotionally to our crush and this makes it very hard when we find he doesn't return the interest, especially if he likes some other girl. It is likely Hannah will waste lots of time and energy dreaming about James, hoping in vain for something that may never happen. What would it take for Hannah to risk surrendering her desire for James to God? It is scary taking your hands off the driving wheel of life. Surrendering the control even to an all loving, all knowing, all powerful God carries the risk we might not get what we want. I remember the moment God asked me to stop fantasy dating and let go of everyone I thought had potential. He stripped me back to just Jesus and me with no other possibilities for as long as he wanted. I felt very insecure about taking the step of total surrender but once I yielded I discovered it to be a very freeing thing. Instead of worrying about why my fantasy date doesn't notice me I think, "God will bring it together without my help if it is meant to be" which enables me to treat young men as brothers in Christ instead of potential husbands. No longer do I look at young men and wonder "is he THE ONE?" It took so much energy trying to work everything out based on my own understanding. Now I rest in the comfort that God is holding my heart and he will show me the right one at the right time.

Here is a helpful tip, if you see a cute looking guy walking down the road and your mind begins to wonder if maybe he's THE ONE. To stop your mind building castles in the air (they only lead to disappointment) bounce your eyes. This is similar to the eye bounce you may have heard guys use to stop looking at impure things. If I see a guy that I think is good looking, I will bounce my eyes away and not go for a second look, this has nothing to do with immodesty, it has everything to do with keeping my mind from day dreaming about some random guy, which I believe for me personally, is not something God would want me to do. I am not saying that God wouldn't tell you, who THE ONE is before the guy is interested in you. I am just saying that when we hand the controls of our mind to Christ, there is freedom and peace, knowing that it's not up to us to bring it all together. It is God's will and decision and he is powerful enough to do it. After all he is the one who invented marriage.

How Can We Maintain Purity?

What Others Say

Maintaining your purity is a war. The greatest thing an army can have under fire is a superb leader and the greatest thing they can do, is to completely trust and obey him. Devote your life to God, put him first and he will enable you to win the war.

~Ruth Hamilton~

Reading and meditating on the word of God daily, living out Phil. 4:8

~Evan~

Stay away from situations that could endanger your purity.

~Taylor Stephenson~

Having a relationship with Jesus is the key thing a person can do to maintain ones purity. In today's society there are many distractions and temptations that seem more exciting than the word of God. It is a trick of the enemy to corrupt and contaminate our souls. The Holy Spirit is our helper. When we allow the presence of God to take over our souls we find strength and even gain an appetite for things that are holy and pure. As the Holy Spirit lives in us he acts as a personal guest in our soul. The Holy Spirit will instruct our hearts in what he does and doesn't desire, as the presence of God draws us closer to him.

~Shanaya Sykes~

Seek to walk in the Spirit, stay in God's word, pray, get involved in a bible studyand make a purity pact with friends

~Taylor D~

The Bible says to shun the very appearance of evil. It is not a very smart idea to be in a room alone (be it an office, bedroom or any room) with the door closed with the opposite gender.

~Rachel Nipp~

Put your standards high and stick to them. Don't put yourself in tempting situations. Feed your eyes, ears, mind and heart with positive things that build you up in the word of God

~Maria Leite~

Pray a lot, read the bible and trust GOD.

~Ana Trochez~

Accountability partners are vital. Whether it's a sibling, leader, parent, or friend, we all need another set of eyes to keep us in check. Ecclesiastes 4:9-12 says, "Two are better than one. If one falls, one can help the other up. Though one may be overpowered, two can defend themselves.

~Lianna Joy~

One most important thing is to secure your relationship with God, pray, study his word and surround yourself with Godly people.

~BFA~

The key to maintain purity is Jesus. We are all weak but with Gods strength we can do much!!

~Cynthia Castillo~

Avoid tempting situations and study the word because when you have the spirit of God in you, you're more able to fight impurity.

~Taylor~

Do not put yourself in a tempting situation where it's easy to give in.

~JR~

I think if you state upfront, what your standards are, and do not waiver from them, it's a loteasier, (especially if the guy feels the same way). Reading your Bible and doing your best to be on fire for God helps a lot too.

~ActualGodlyGirl~

I believe the most important thing a person can do to maintain purity is to know what composes their morals. If you know what you believe in, you can stand for it.

~Francesca Dominique C. Jimenez.~

Prayer and accountability are the most important factors when considering the maintenance of purity in someone's life. The more disconnected from God I am, the more likely I am to stray. When I want a trusted friend I can talk to, I'm always brought back to God. He answers our prayers and gives us the strength that we need to endure—we need only ask. So many of us are too ashamed or guilt-ridden to ask for forgiveness, but when we do, freedom comes.

~Aysha Gerald~

Guard your heart!!! Proverbs 4:23 says, "Keep your heart with all diligence, for out of it is the wellspring of life."

~Cherish~

Save any kind of physical intimacy for marriage, don't spend time alone with the opposite gender behind closed doors or in any kind of private setting. Have accountability partners—preferably older and of the same gender—the girl should have an older woman mentor, and the guy should have an older man mentor who keeps them accountable. Pray and spend time each day in God's word and be guarded about what you watch on TV, or listen to or read.

~Erika Cockerham~

The key thing a person can do to maintain their purity is to keep their heart right with God.

~Ruth England~

Courting Or Dating Does It Matter?

―――――――――― ∽Ↄᴇ ᴐↄ∾ ――――――――――

Trust in the Lord with all your heart and lean not on your own understanding; in all your ways submit to him, and he will make your paths straight. Proverbs 3:5-6

HERE IS A BEACH NOT far from us that is a picturesque little bay. In summer the water is very blue and sparkles invitingly. What I didn't know about that nice little swimming spot is that underneath that smooth surface is lots of sharp little rocks. Also the camp at the water's edge has problems with its septic system. The unwary soon find out like I did, that it takes months to clear up the nasty sores acquired from one swim. In matters of the heart it is easy to get so caught up focusing on surface matters that we forget to look at the deeper issues. Many people think dating is a normal way of life. Others are convinced dating is wrong, that courtship is the better option and some cultures believe arranged marriages are the best, where your parents chose who you marry. I believe all of these ways are valid they are just like the sparkly blue water. What matters most is are you willing to do whatever God asks you to do, or are you just looking for the best and fastest way to get your man. I have friends who dated, some who courted and others whose marriage was arranged, and they are all happily married. I know of ones that didn't work out either. God wants you to put him first, he sees your heart and doesn't want you to get side tracked by some preconceived formula. Not everyone will understand the path God has mapped out for you, especially if it differs from the normal practice of your culture. But it's going to be amazing and beautiful because he is writing your love story. He knows the special plans he has for you and can keep your heart away from sharp rocks.

Attraction or Reaction

But test everything; hold fast what is good. 1 Thessalonians 5:21

LAURA HADN'T EVEN LIKED PHIL when she first met him. "He's a flirt and he likes having girls worship him" she complained to her mother one Sunday. "I don't see how anyone could like him." Everyone knew of Laura's distain for him, including Phil and suddenly she seemed very attractive to him. Soon he was sitting by her at lunch, sending her beautiful cards and flowers and all together turning on the charm and slowly but surely Laura's true feelings about him were pushed aside. She began to fall for him. One day when she was giggling over some silly text he had sent her, her mother said "Laura I thought you hated Phil." "Yeah, I did, but he's different now." Laura sighed dreamily. "I feel so attracted to him, he shall be my prince and I his princess."

My sister always thought all dogs were smelly and yucky, until a dog showed interest in her, and it didn't stop with one dog. Soon it seemed as if she had captured the heart of the entire dog population. When she went to the beach, dogs would come running to meet her. Dogs would even leave their owners to come to her and guess what? My sister

Rachel Hamilton

really loves and adores dogs now. This can be the same with relationships. You meet someone you don't really notice but they notice you and start taking an interest in you. And just like Laura and my sister, your whole view changes because you are so flattered that someone would actually like you. Suddenly Bozo changes into Mr Smooth. This could be nothing more than a reaction. Flattery is a flimsy emotion to hang a marriage on and so is the idea "well no one else would want me, better take what I can get."

If you are meant to marry there is someone out there who will love you with all their heart, don't sell yourself short. I used to think that if someone liked me that I had to like them back.

When a house is for sale the Real Estate Agent puts up large yellow signs sometimes with the amusing wording of "Buyer Wanted", which is rather stating the obvious. Only a fool would rush in and buy the first house they saw because the Agent was flatteringly interested in them and the house was blatantly available. In the same way you don't have to marry the first person who shows interest in you. I am not saying God couldn't bring you a husband this way, he could. I am just saying that we need to be careful not to fall for someone purely on the basis that he showed interest in us. We should carefully look for lots of common interests and values and pray about it before we start into a relationship because marriage needs to be grounded on so much more than a reaction to attraction.

I Love Him Because I'm Lonely

One who is full loathes honey from the comb,
but to the hungry even what is bitter tastes sweet.
Proverbs 27:7

MELANIE WASN'T LOOKING FOR A summer romance during her gap year in Italy, but there must have been something in the air that fateful night at the quaint little cafe, when a tall dark stranger asked if he could sit at her table. There was something comforting about having a man next to her, so she agreed. Melanie had been very lonely since she had left home, the novelty of being on her own had quickly worn off and she felt insecure and small. Little did she know that over next few weeks she would become close to the tall dark stranger. What a perfect love story or is it? Have you ever felt lonely in the middle of a crowd like Melanie? You just want someone to notice and like you for yourself. It is even harder when you are surrounded by couples. Everyone has someone but you. As girls we often long for someone strong to sense when we feel insecure, to sooth our fears and say I will protect you.

While I believe that this is a God given desire, we must be so careful not to fall for someone through vulnerability. Just because he put a strong hand on your shoulder when you needed it, doesn't mean he is THE ONE. Of course this could be the way God wants you to meet, but we must guard against falling into emotional entanglement just because he acted like a man.

Not so very long ago God put me in a place where I was very vulnerable, he sent me to a place where I was emotionally abused, I was isolated and I longed for a young man who could strengthen and comfort me. But that wasn't the best for me. If God had brought someone into my life then, I may have made a wrong decision because he made me feel safe, I may have been deafened to Gods voice saying he wasn't he one. I may have read a lot more into the situation and thought, "Well he must be the one because God brought him when I needed him the most."

God knows what's best even if it doesn't feel like it. It has really helps to step back and ask the question," do I like this guy because I am lonely and tired of being alone or is there more to my feelings about him?" God will give us wisdom and guidance if we ask him. So ask him to show you and he will guide you.

To Those Who Have Lost Their Purity

What Others Say

God doesn't rate sin on a curve. We do, but he doesn't. Lustful sin is a sin. A horrible sin and it makes God sad, but it doesn't sit in a special unforgivable category. Nothing you do can ever put you outside the power of God's forgiveness or love.

~Ruth Hamilton~

God is a gracious God who can make all things anew in life (: Second chances and hope come from Him.

~Rachel Sophieanne~c

It's never too late to restore your purity. If that's truly what you want in your heart, God will restore and renew you

~Maddi Mae~

God forgives and he still accepts you for all your flaws. Anyone can be washed clean through God's forgiveness because God renews and restores!

~Brooke~

Purity can still be achieved. Isaiah 1:18 says our sins are washed white as snow, giving us a second chance in The Lord. In Him we are a new creation, our past is behind us.

~Taylor D~

God still loves them as much as He used to, there is nothing anyone can do to make God love them more or less. God is a restorer.

~Tinashe Nyahasha~

GOD loves you and will forgive you. He will heal your heart, let him take control of your life.

~Ana Trochez~

Once, I met this boy in church. We started spending time together alone, and having deeply personal conversations about our spiritual lives as well as our pasts. After a while, we started what seemed like harmless flirting and started texting each other when we weren't together. Needless to say, we both lost our focus on God. One night, when we were alone, our first kiss went too far. We didn't go all the way, but our actions weren't pure. He didn't talk to me for weeks afterwards, and I was extremely hurt and confused. Until then, I didn't realize how much I cared for him, not just romantically, but as a friend. I thought he felt the same. When I saw him

at church, he ignored me and when I texted him about it, he excused himself as being busy. Finally, one day after church, he apologized for hurting my feelings and misleading me. He never intended to have a relationship with me. I apologized for any behaviour that might've induced our sin. I stopped attending the bible study and we never attempted to see each other again. Not only did we destroy our "friendship", we sinned against God, ourselves, and each other. I felt worthless, rejected, and guilty. It was a long road to healing. It seemed God was far away, but I clung to his promises and grace, and I drew near to him again. These three passages comforted me immensely: Luke 7:37-50 talks about Jesus forgiving a harlot. Isaiah 61:3 talks about God giving "beauty for ashes" and "joy for mourning". Isaiah 54:5-8 talks about God's great forgiveness and how he will welcome back Israel, his unfaithful bride, with loving arms. I completely re-evaluated my personal convictions when it came to purity after that experience. I always thought that going after guys was okay as long as I stayed a virgin until marriage, I'd be fine. It took falling hard for someone and getting hurt to realize purity isn't just not sinning—it's giving God your whole heart so that you are no longer interested in even coming close to sin. I'd tell anyone who has lost their purity that, through our great God, they can get it back. ("Though your sins are like scarlet, they shall be as white as snow" Isaiah 1:18) and that God can use our biggest downfalls to make us wiser and to reveal himself to us even more.

~Lianna Joy~

To someone who has lost their purity, I say "you do not have to work for grace God loves you, and can make you whole and pure again."

~Waiting for your Boaz~

That God is a forgiving God and you can receive forgiveness and comfort from Him. Even though you gave yourself away, you can repent and become pure again.

~Taylor~

God is a God of second chances, He can redeem and heal you.

~ActualGodlyGirl~

God is not caught off guard! He knew before you were born, that you would lose your purity! He still loves you, and has good plans for your life! Your story could help other people, and encourage them to keep their purity safe. Learn from this, and use it as part of your testimony.

~Cherish~

Well, since I lost my purity before I received the Lord, I can encourage you by saying it is okay. Once you come to Christ, He washes you of all of your sins and shame, and He clothes you with a holy garment. Your past doesn't define you, Christ defines you. You are reborn, and pure before God. Let your past be a testimony that glorifies God.

~Julia Grace~

There is nothing we can do to make God stop loving us, or to make Him refuse to forgive us. God loves us and redeems us and it is because of Christ's sacrifice on the cross that we don't have to live in condemnation and can be set free from our sin.

~Erika Cockerham~

The most comforting thing I can say to someone who has lost their purity would be "God is still on the throne. Get right with Him. If you ask God to forgive you and help you get your purity back He will. And don't let anyone judge you because of this".

~Ruth England~

When we give our lives to God, we're new. He makes us new. Therefore, we can reclaim our purity.

~Chanell Washington~

Yes. All things are made new. I believe in being what I call a "born-again virgin".

~Yeisie Marie~

Yes I do believe it's possible to reclaim your purity. While I am no longer a virgin, I have been celibate and am walking in Christ. Being celibate is not what makes me pure and if I was a virgin, it wouldn't mean I'd automatically be pure in Gods eyes. I believe that giving my heart to Jesus and following all his commandments whole heartedly is what makes me pure and is what will make any individual in any struggle pure. I've accepted Jesus Christ as my personal Lord and Saviour and his blood has cleansed me and every day I strive to ensure a holy lifestyle so that my mind, body and spirit are pure before a pure and holy God!

~Shanaya Sykes~

Through Jesus Christ, nothing is impossible. He can wash you clean again.

~Maria Leite~

Yes it is possible to reclaim lost purity. True purity comes from the blood of Jesus. Without Jesus, no matter "how good" anyone is, they remain filthy. After being washed by his blood, we become accepted no matter what we did in the past.

~Tinashe Nyahasha~

Oh yes! It is very possible to reclaim your purity. God is a God of second chances. I was abused as a child but I always say to people close to me that I am a virgin. At first I was just living in denial but now I know better. I have been cleaned up and made new. I am sure I will find how true my belief is when I get married.

~BFA~

I lost my purity and it hurt. But God redeemed me I am no longer stained but white as snow :) Thanks to the blood of Jesus!

~Cynthia Castillo~

I definitely believe it's possible to reclaim purity. I think it's a choice that we make, each and every day, to surrender our thoughts, desires, wants, and wishes to God. That doesn't mean that we will always do it right, but it's the decision to wake up in the morning and say, "God, today I need your strength to be pure of mind, heart, and body. You've called me to be a light to others, and my prayer is that this temple would be used for your glory." He will always give us everything we need in the moment that we need it. We just have to want it.

~Aysha Gerald~

Yes. Physical purity can be lost, but spiritual purity comes when you know the Most High and surrender your life to Him. I was a terrible sinner, but Jesus came and restored to me my purity, and I am dressed in white ready for the wedding feast.

~Julia Grace~

I do believe it's possible, because I know God is a redeeming God and the Great Healer and Restorer. There is no sin bad enough to keep God from healing and restoring someone who repented and had a genuine heart follow God.

However, even though God can forgive and heal, I don't think sinning is worth any of the consequences one must face if they choose to walk outside the will of God.

~Erika Cockerham~

God is a God of miracles, nothing is impossible! His mercy is good enough to restore everything. There are testimonies from girls who call themselves 'recycled-virgins'. I love the word!

~Lisanne Slotman~

Yesterday, today and tomorrow, Jesus is the same, He still heals and restores.

~Gea Slotman~

The Power of Touch

I charge you, O ye daughters of Jerusalem, by the roes, and by the hinds of the field, that ye stir not up, nor awake my love, till he please. Song of Solomon 2:7

KATE DIDN'T EVEN REALLY NOTICE red headed Cameron Stewart who was part of her summer outreach team, when he sat down at her table for breakfast one morning., They talked pleasantly about the weather and other trivial nothings, over toast and coffee, but as Cameron got up to leave, he touched Kate softly on the shoulder before departing. Over the next few days Kate caught her-self looking for him at meal times, she felt close to him and wanted to get to know him better. Then one day she overheard him talking to a friend about how he missed his girlfriend. Kate was crushed, there was nothing going on between them at all. The power of touch is incredible, a God given thing for the right time. But we must be so careful with touch before we are married. Be very cautious with touching guys and letting them touch you. I am not talking about inappropriate and sinful touch, which of course you must totally avoid. I am talking about touches on the shoulder, shoulder massages, leaning on you. I don't believe these are necessarily sinful but it is such a powerful thing between a man and woman that it can awaken something in you and give you a false sense of closeness. Sometimes when a guy goes around touching us in a casual friendly way we mistakenly believe he likes us more then he really does. Like Kate we can read too much into things, thinking about a situation over and over again which he forgot long ago. It may be enjoyable and flattering when a guy hugs you and rests his head on your shoulder, but too much of this can emotionally bond you to the wrong person.

There are countless movies of boys and girls kissing, even as young as twelve. It is so sad to see what little respect the media gives the power of touch. The media sends a strong message that seventeen and never-been-kissed equals something wrong with you. At twenty-one and never-been-kissed, I can tell you, that I have been saved a lot of heartache and emotional entanglement. Touch between a man and woman when it is the wrong person or wrong time is a dangerous thing. When we are in a relationship but not yet married we must be highly wary of how powerful touch is. Prayerfully with self control guard our hearts and hands so we will fall in love with the mind and the spirit of another person without the distraction of touch with its power to gloss over glaring incompatibilities. So how much touch is too much. It's not about a set of rules but rather it is a heart issue and a relationship issue. Not your relationship with another person but your relationship with God. Do you deep down put Jesus first in every area of your life? Then being pure and accountable in this area will be not any different. If you and the man you like esteem one another's purity in the highest place, then God will help you keep pure with your touch.

Never A Bride

I want you to be free from anxieties. The unmarried man is anxious about the things of the Lord, how to please the Lord. 1 Corinthians 7:32

W E HAVE LOTS OF WORLD-CLASS mountains in the South Island of New Zealand that attract lots of climbers. The land spreads out from the coast as plains for a little and then rises steeply into the Southern Alps. We must be the only country in the world where it is possible to ski in the morning and go to the beach in the afternoon. No matter how wonderful the mountains in New Zealand are, the ultimate challenge for a climber will always be Mount Everest. I guess all mountain climbers must wonder "will I ever climb Everest?" At this stage of life the big question in all of our hearts is not "will I climb Everest' but "will I ever marry"? Here is a challenge. Will you keep trusting God if he never brings you a husband? Will you still do whatever Christ asks you to do even if it means you will never marry? Can you even face the question or do you believe God must bring you a husband or he doesn't love you? Some decisions are like jumping off a water fall, once you've jumped there is no chance changing of your mind. For me deciding to follow Christ even if he never fulfils my desire to marry is more like giving up chocolate. I think I have given my all to God and then like the craving for the chocolate in the fridge, the roller coaster ride of emotional longings starts up again and I have to lay everything down once more. If I am truly surrendered to God I have to face the unpleasant possibility that marriage may not be Gods highest calling for me, singleness could be what he has in store for me. True surrender means we can request things from God but he has the right to say "No I have something better in store for you." If I never marry it doesn't mean that God loves me any less than the people who marry. No it means that he has a special unusual plan for my life and he will compensate by making it a very fulfilling path.

It doesn't mean that I will never have longings, but Gods will is always the very best place to be, no matter what it is. You could fill a library with books written about bad marriages and ruined lives through disobeying God, but I have never yet heard of anyone who said "I obeyed God and really regret it." I have an Aunty who would like to have married but that has not been part of God's plan for her so far. She is now in her fifties and leads a vibrant fulfilling life because she has never put her life on hold waiting for a husband neither has she complicated it with the messy baggage of sinful living. She is a school teacher with a great social life who regularly leads mission trips around the world and makes the most of the freedom of her singleness.

She is a great example of how trusting God whether you are married or single to give you a life full of meaning. Sometimes I wonder would I be able to cope as a single person my whole life. Then I remember I have coped being single for twenty one years and my Aunty for over fifty years so I know God could get me through another sixty odd years if that was his will. I think the biggest question for a Christian is not "will I ever marry" but "will I always obey?"

Thanks

HEARTFELT THANKS TO EVERYONE AT WestBow Press who has made my dream come true. Thank you so much to Randy Clayton, John Osredker and Sarah Davis you have made the publishing process so easy and enjoyable.

A special thanks to my parents Ian and Wendy Hamilton. You are the best parents that I could ask for. Thank you so much for always supporting me and showing me what a godly marriage looks like and for helping bring this book together.

Thank you so much to my sister Ruth Hamilton, you are an amazing woman of God, thank you so much for being such a godly role model, thank you for always standing for what's right. Special thanks to my great brothers Paul and John Hamilton. We always have so much fun together. Love you so much!

Thank you so much Mr and Mrs Williams for being such wonderful friends to me over the years.

A huge thanks to Rebecca Williams, Emily Williams, Susanna Williams and Sharday Noon, I am so blessed by your friendship and thank you so much for all your help with this book, I couldn't have done it without you.

My amazing ship friends and friends from Sri Lanka you have touched my life in a deep way. Also my amazing friend and cabin mate Sarah Sonneveld thanks for being an answer to prayer.

Thank you so much Lisanne Slotman for all your help and encouragement and for your great ideas. I couldn't have done it without you. You are such a blessing.

Thanks so much to True Love Waits Philippines ministry, for all your help and support.

Huge thanks to all my Facebook and Twitter followers who kindly let me quote them.

Allie Jolley, Peyton Wilpot, ToMyLovingWife, Austin Abernathy, Megan Marie, BFA, Erin Wood Young Man's Struggle, Lily Jones, Taylor Devine, Rachel Nipp, Tinashe Nyahasha, Jesse, Shanaya Sykes, Tips4ChristiansTeens, Hannah Patulski, Lianna Joy, Ana Trochez, Maria Leite Emily Diehl, Keyshana Coleman, Jawoeh Kerrt, Charmaine Garica Anac, Toritomone, Christianbelle0, David Donegan, Annie Trochez, Juliee, Jess Lacy, Cherish, Cynthia Castillo, Emily D, Taylor, JR, ActualGodlyGirl, Julia Grace, Erika Lopez, Cheri Joyner, Raelynn Russell, Princess Pink, Carolyn Krolick, Aysha Gerald, Nancy Aneke, Shikussimon Tode, Fancessa Jemenez, Colette, Gabrielle Kinnish, Lisanne Slotman, Brandy Reed, Kassandra Wiseley, Jennifer Passet, Karin Uys, Carolina Mukami, Ganiya Tairu, Kamal Kumar, Erika Cockerham, Edher Cavero Joseph J, Ruth England, Chimwemwe Mtamba, Nathan Kochler, Chelsea Chappell, Kaylin Cassity Brooke, Hasten Home, InChristAlone, Sanet, Chelsey Pennington, Nina Haaskivi, Taylor Stephenson, Alex Christian, SouthernProverbs31, Edin, Josh Collins, King Mufasa, Josbel Nazario, Joshua Nason, I-AM-TOBRIN-FROST, Rebecca, Chris Blankenship, Catherine Martinez, WhyWontYouWait, Maddi Mae, Countrybaptist, Anonymous, Rachel MoeyPatricia, Generation 31, Classy Gal, Christian

Gent, Andra Jimenez, Adedamola Tinubu Bur, Actual Gentlmen, Michael Germain, Richard Jay, Richard T, Gea Slotman, Sierra Palacios Lisanne Slotman, A teen girls heart, Rebekah Caldwell, Jenn Rosario, Hadlee Hamner, Rachel Sophieanne, Bisantio Anthony, Evan, Chanell Washington, Yelsie marie, Disney princess 4 God, Northern Gentleman, Chris Evangelista, Jordan Azpanta, Ronnel Ramos, Rm Rodriquez, Mark Soriano, Paul Placer, Arvick Mirondo. I am so sorry if I missed any names out it was unintentional. Thank you so much to everyone who sent me quotes for this book, gave me advice and support, I really sorry I couldn't include everyone but I loved reading and hearing your insight! May God bless you all so much!

Thank you to God who never left me and who makes the impossible possible, to Him be the glory, for in him alone my hope is found.

About the Author

————⬡⬡⬡————

RACHEL HAMILTON IS A NEW Zealand writer. The founder of 'It's Worth the Wait. Becoming God's Men and Women in Waiting,' an online ministry to encourage those waiting for God's best. Through Facebook, Twitter and YouTube, she aims to help people see that they are not alone and that God has amazing plans for their lives.

Find out more about her ministry
Facebook: facebook/Godswomaninwaiting
Twitter: @waitingisbest
Visit her blog rachelhamiltonnz.wordpress.com

Printed in Australia
AUOC01n1532311017
291047AU00001B/1/P